THE MAYOR OF CASTERBRIDGE

Thomas Hardy

TECHNICAL DIRECTOR Maxwell Krohn
EDITORIAL DIRECTOR Justin Kestler
MANAGING EDITOR Ben Florman

SERIES EDITORS Boomie Aglietti, Justin Kestler
PRODUCTION Christian Lorentzen

WRITERS Rebecca Gaines, David Hopson
EDITORS Benjamin Morgan, Dennis Quinio

This edition published by Spark Publishing

Spark Publishing
A Division of SparkNotes LLC
120 Fifth Avenue, 8th Floor
New York, NY 10011

02 03 04 05 SN 9 8 7 6 5 4 3 2 1

Please send all comments and questions or report errors to
feedback@sparknotes.com.

Library of Congress information available upon request

Printed and bound in the United States

RRD-C

ISBN 1-58663-479-8

Introduction: Stopping to Buy Sparknotes on a Snowy Evening

Whose words these are you *think* you know.
Your paper's due tomorrow, though;
We're glad to see you stopping here
To get some help before you go.

Lost your course? You'll find it here.
Face tests and essays without fear.
Between the words, good grades at stake:
Get great results throughout the year.

Once school bells caused your heart to quake
As teachers circled each mistake.
Use SparkNotes and no longer weep,
Ace every single test you take.

Yes, books are lovely, dark, and deep,
But only what you grasp you keep,
With hours to go before you sleep,
With hours to go before you sleep.

Contents

NOTE: This SparkNote refers to the second edition of the Norton Critical Edition of *The Mayor of Casterbridge*, which is based on the Macmillan Wessex Edition of 1912. The novel varies significantly based on the publication's origin (United States or Britain) and style (book form or serial).

CONTEXT

THOMAS HARDY WAS BORN on June 2, 1840, in Higher Bockhampton in Dorset, a rural region of southwestern England that was to become the focus of his fiction. The child of a builder, Hardy was apprenticed at the age of sixteen to John Hicks, an architect who lived in the city of Dorchester. The location would later serve as the model for Hardy's fictional Casterbridge. Although Hardy gave serious thought to attending university and entering the church, a struggle he would dramatize in his 1895 novel *Jude the Obscure,* his declining religious faith and lack of money encouraged him to pursue a career in writing instead. Hardy spent nearly a dozen years toiling in obscurity and producing unsuccessful novels and poetry. *Far from the Madding Crowd,* published in 1874, was his first critical and financial success. Finally able to support himself as a writer, Hardy married Emma Lavinia Gifford later that year.

Although he built a reputation as a successful novelist, Hardy considered himself—first and foremost—a poet. To him, novels were primarily a means of earning a living. Like many novelists of his day, he wrote according to the conventions of serialization (the process of publishing a work in periodic installments). To insure that readers would buy a serialized novel, writers often left pressing questions unanswered at the end of each installment. This practice explains the convoluted, often incredible plots of many nineteenth-century Victorian novels. But Hardy cannot be labeled solely a Victorian novelist. Nor can he be categorized as purely a modernist, in the tradition of writers like Virginia Woolf or D. H. Lawrence who were determined to explode the conventions of nineteenth-century literature and build a new kind of novel in its place. In many respects, Hardy was trapped between the nineteenth and twentieth centuries, between Victorian and modern sensibilities, and between tradition and innovation.

The Mayor of Casterbridge reveals Hardy's peculiar location in this shifting world, possessing elements of both the Victorian and modernist forms. It charts the course of one man's character, but it also chronicles the dramatic change of an isolated, rural agricultural community into a modern city. In *The Mayor of Casterbridge,* as well as in his most popular fictions, such as *Tess of the D'Urbervilles* and *Jude the Obscure,* Hardy explores the effects of cultural and economic development: the decline of Christianity as well as folk traditions, the rise of industrialization and urbanization, and the unraveling of universally held moral codes.

Hardy himself abandoned Christianity. He read the writings of Charles Darwin, accepted the theory of evolution, and studied the German philosopher Arthur Schopenhauer. Schopenhauer's notion of the "Immanent Will" describes a blind force that drives the universe irrespective of human lives or desires. Though his novels often end in crushing tragedies that reflect Schopenhauer's philosophy, Hardy described himself as a *meliorist,* one who believes that the world tends to become better and that people aid in this betterment. Humans can live with some happiness, he claimed, so long as they understand their place in the universe and accept it. Hardy died in 1928 at his estate in Dorchester. True to the rather dramatically romantic fantasies of his fiction, Hardy had his heart buried in his wife's tomb.

Plot Overview

ICHAEL HENCHARD IS TRAVELING with his wife, Susan, looking for employment as a hay-trusser. When they stop to eat, Henchard gets drunk, and in an auction that begins as a joke but turns serious, he sells his wife and their baby daughter, Elizabeth-Jane, to Newson, a sailor, for five guineas. In the morning, Henchard regrets what he has done and searches the town for his wife and daughter. Unable to find them, he goes into a church and swears an oath that he will not drink alcohol for twenty-one years, the same number of years he has been alive.

After the sailor's death, eighteen years later, Susan and Elizabeth-Jane seek Henchard; Elizabeth-Jane believes he is merely a long-lost relative. They arrive in Casterbridge and learn that Henchard is the mayor. The parents meet and decide that in order to prevent Elizabeth-Jane from learning of their disgrace, Henchard will court and remarry Susan as though they had met only recently.

Meanwhile, Henchard has hired Donald Farfrae, a young Scotchman, as the new manager of his corn business. Elizabeth-Jane is intrigued by Farfrae, and the two begin to spend time together. Henchard becomes alienated from Farfrae, however, as the younger man consistently outdoes Henchard in every respect. He asks Farfrae to leave his business and to stop courting Elizabeth-Jane.

Susan falls ill and dies soon after her remarriage to Henchard. After discovering that Elizabeth-Jane is not his own daughter, but Newson's, Henchard becomes increasingly cold toward her. Elizabeth-Jane then decides to leave Henchard's house and live with a lady who has just arrived in town. This lady turns out to be Lucetta Templeman, a woman with whom Henchard was involved during Susan's absence; having learned of Susan's death, Lucetta has come to Casterbridge to marry Henchard.

While Lucetta is waiting for Henchard to call on her, she meets Farfrae, who has come to call on Elizabeth-Jane. The two hit it off and are eventually married. Lucetta asks Henchard to return to her all the letters she has sent him. On his way to deliver the letters, the messenger, Jopp, stops at an inn. The peasants there convince him to open and read the letters aloud. Discovering that Lucetta and Henchard have been romantically involved, the peasants decide to hold a "skimmity-ride," a humiliating parade portraying Lucetta and Henchard together. The event takes place one afternoon when Farfrae is away. Lucetta faints upon seeing the spectacle and becomes very ill. Shortly afterward, she dies.

While Henchard has grown to hate Farfrae, he has grown closer to Elizabeth-Jane. The morning after Lucetta's death, Newson, who is actually still alive, arrives at Henchard's door and asks for Elizabeth-Jane. Henchard tells him that she is dead, and Newson leaves in sorrow. Elizabeth-Jane stays with Henchard and also begins to spend more time with Farfrae. One day, Henchard learns that Newson has returned to town, and he decides to leave rather than risk another confrontation. Elizabeth-Jane is reunited with Newson and learns of Henchard's deceit; Newson and Farfrae start planning the wedding between Elizabeth-Jane and the Scotchman.

Henchard comes back to Casterbridge on the night of the wedding to see Elizabeth-Jane, but she snubs him. He leaves again, telling her that he will not return. She soon regrets her coldness, and she and Farfrae, her new husband, go looking for Henchard so that she can make her peace. Unfortunately, they find him too late, discovering that he has died alone in the countryside. He has left a will: his dying wish is to be forgotten.

CHARACTER LIST

Michael Henchard As the novel's protagonist, Henchard is the "Man of Character" to whom the subtitle of *The Mayor of Casterbridge* alludes. When the novel opens, Henchard is a disconsolate twenty-one-year-old hay-trusser who, in a drunken rage, sells his wife and daughter at a county fair. Eighteen years later, Henchard has risen to become the mayor and the most accomplished corn merchant in the town of Casterbridge. Although he tries to atone for his youthful crimes, he focuses too much on his past misdeeds and enters a downward trajectory that embroils him in a fierce competition with a popular Scotchman named Donald Farfrae.

Elizabeth-Jane Newson The daughter of Susan and Newson. Elizabeth-Jane bears the same name as the child born to Susan and Henchard, who actually dies shortly after Henchard sells Susan and his daughter. Over the course of the novel, the independent and self-possessed Elizabeth-Jane transforms herself from an unrefined country girl into a cultured young lady. Though she experiences much hardship over the course of the novel, she maintains an even temperament throughout.

Donald Farfrae The Scotchman who arrives in Casterbridge at the same time as Susan Henchard and Elizabeth-Jane. Farfrae's business efficiency, good humor, and polish make him extremely popular among the town's citizens. These same qualities, however, eventually make him Henchard's rival. Despite this tension in their friendship, Farfrae remains fair-minded, patient, and even kind in his dealings with the ruined Henchard.

Lucetta Templeman A woman whom Henchard meets, courts, and proposes to marry. Lucetta bucks convention, choosing to love whom she pleases when she pleases. Like Henchard, she is guided by her emotions, and her reactions are thus not always rational.

Susan Henchard A meek, unassuming woman married to Michael Henchard when the novel opens. Overly concerned with propriety, Susan attempts to keep secrets about Henchard's and Elizabeth-Jane's identities in order to give the appearance of perfect family harmony.

Newson The sailor who buys Susan and Elizabeth-Jane from Henchard. Newson is absent for most of the novel; his eventual reappearance contributes to the feeling that Henchard is besieged by fate.

Joshua Jopp The man Henchard intends to hire as his assistant before meeting Farfrae.

Abel Whittle One of the workers in Henchard's hay-yard. Whittle is also the source of the first disagreement between Henchard and Farfrae, as Farfrae thinks that Henchard is too rough with Whittle when he is constantly late for work.

Benjamin Grower One of Henchard's creditors.

Christopher Coney A peasant in Casterbridge. Coney represents the bleak reality of peasant life.

Nance Mockridge A peasant who is instrumental in planning the skimmity-ride.

Mother Cuxsom A peasant in Casterbridge.

Solomon Longways A peasant in Casterbridge.

ANALYSIS OF MAJOR CHARACTERS

MICHAEL HENCHARD

At the end of *The Mayor of Casterbridge*, the ruined Michael Henchard wills that no one remember his name after his death. This request is profoundly startling and tragic, especially when one considers how important Henchard's name has been to him during his lifetime. After committing the abominable deed of selling his wife and child, Henchard wakes from a drunken stupor and wonders, first and foremost, if he told any of the fair-goers his name. Eighteen years pass between that scene on the heath of Weydon-Priors and Henchard's reunion with Susan in Casterbridge, but we immediately realize the value that Henchard places on a good name and reputation. Not only has he climbed from hay-trusser to mayor of a small agricultural town, but he labors to protect the esteem this higher position affords him. When Susan and Elizabeth-Jane come upon the mayor hosting a banquet for the town's most prominent citizens, they witness a man struggling to convince the masses that, despite a mismanaged harvest, he is an honest person with a worthy name.

As he stares out at an unhappy audience made up of grain merchants who have lost money and common citizens who, without wheat, are going hungry, Henchard laments that he cannot undo the past. He relates grown wheat metaphorically to the mistakes of the past—neither can be taken back. Although Henchard learns this lesson at the end of Chapter IV, he fails to internalize it. If there is, indeed, a key to his undoing, it is his inability to let go of his past mistakes. Guilt acts like a fuel that keeps Henchard moving toward his own demise. Unable to forget the events that took place in the furmity-woman's tent, he sets out to punish himself again and again. While he might have found happiness by marrying Lucetta, for instance, Henchard determines to make amends for the past by remarrying a woman he never loved in the first place. Possessed of a "restless and self-accusing soul," Henchard seems to seek out situations that promise further debasement. Although Donald Farfrae eventually appropriates Henchard's job, business, and even his loved ones, it is Henchard who insists on creating the competition that he eventually loses. Although Henchard loses even the ability to explain himself—"he did not sufficiently value himself to lessen his sufferings by strenuous appeal or elaborate argument"—he never relinquishes his talent of endurance. Whatever the pain, Henchard bears it. It is this resilience that elevates him to the level of a hero— a man, ironically, whose name deserves to be remembered.

DONALD FARFRAE

Farfrae, the young Scotchman, serves as a foil (a character whose actions or emotions contrast with and thereby accentuate those of another character) for Henchard. Whereas will and intuition determine the course of Henchard's life, Farfrae is a man of intellect. He brings to Casterbridge a method for salvaging damaged grain, a system for reorganizing and revolutionizing the mayor's business, and a blend of curiosity and ambition that enables him to take interest in—and advantage of—the agricultural advancements of the day (such as the seed-sowing machine).

Although Henchard soon comes to view Farfrae as his adversary, the Scotchman's victories are won more in the name of progress than personal satisfaction. His primary motive in taking over Casterbridge's grain trade is to make it more prosperous and prepare the village for the advancing agricultural economy of the later nineteenth century. He does not intend to dishonor Henchard. Indeed, even when Henchard is at his most adversarial—during his fight with Farfrae in the barn, for instance—the Scotchman reminds himself of the fallen mayor's circumstances, taking pains to understand and excuse Henchard's behavior. In his calm, measured thinking, Farfrae is a model man of science, and Hardy depicts him with the stereotypical strengths and weaknesses of such people. He possesses an intellectual competence so unrivaled that it passes for charisma, but throughout the novel he remains emotionally distant. Although he wins the favor of the townspeople with his highly successful day of celebration, Farfrae fails to feel any emotion too deeply, whether it is happiness inspired by his carnival or sorrow at the death of his wife. In this respect as well he stands in bold contrast to Henchard, whose depth of feeling is so profound that it ultimately dooms him.

ELIZABETH-JANE NEWSON

Elizabeth-Jane undergoes a drastic transformation over the course of the novel, even though the narrative does not focus on her as much as it does on other characters. As she follows her mother across the English countryside in search of a relative she does not know, Elizabeth-Jane proves a kind, simple, and uneducated girl. Once in Casterbridge, however, she undertakes intellectual and social improvement: she begins to dress like a lady, reads voraciously, and does her best to expunge rustic country dialect from her speech. This self-education comes at a painful time, for not long after she arrives in Casterbridge, her mother dies, leaving her in the custody of a man who has learned that she is not his biological daughter and therefore wants little to do with her.

In terms of misery, one could easily argue that Elizabeth-Jane has a share equal to that of Henchard or Lucetta. Unlike these characters, however, Elizabeth-Jane suffers in the same way she lives—with a quiet kind of self-possession and resolve. She lacks Lucetta's sense of drama and lacks her stepfather's desire to bend the will of others to her own. Thus, when Henchard cruelly dismisses her or Lucetta supplants her place in Farfrae's heart, Elizabeth-Jane accepts these circumstances and moves on with life. This approach to living stands as a bold counterpoint to Henchard's, for Henchard cannot bring himself to let go of the past and relinquish his failures and unfulfilled desires. If Henchard's determination to cling to the past is partly responsible for his ruin, then Elizabeth-Jane's talent for "making limited opportunities endurable" accounts for her triumphal realization—unspectacular as it might be—that "happiness was but the occasional episode in a general drama of pain."

LUCETTA TEMPLEMAN

Like Michael Henchard, Lucetta Templeman lives recklessly according to her passions and suffers for it. Before arriving in Casterbridge, Lucetta becomes involved in a scandalously indiscreet affair with Henchard that makes her the pariah of Jersey. After settling in High-Place Hall, Lucetta quickly becomes enamored with Henchard's archrival, Farfrae. Their relationship is peaceful until the town learns of Lucetta's past relationship with Henchard, whereupon they make her the subject of a shameful "skimmity-ride." Although warned of these likely consequences, Lucetta proceeds to love whomever she wants however she pleases. Still, her character lacks the boldness and certainty of purpose that would elevate her to the level of "the isolated, damned, and self-destructive individualist" that critic Albert Guerard describes as "the great nineteenth-century myth." Lucetta emerges not as heroic but as childish and imprudent. Her love for Farfrae, for example, hinges on her refusal to accept Henchard's visits for several days, a refusal that makes her seem more petty than resolute. Similarly, her rapidly shifting affections—Farfrae eclipses Henchard as the object of her desire with amazing, almost ridiculous speed—brand her as an emotionally volatile Victorian female, one whose sentiments are strong enough to cause the most melodramatic of deaths.

THEMES, MOTIFS & SYMBOLS

THEMES

Themes are the fundamental and often universal ideas explored in a literary work.

THE IMPORTANCE OF CHARACTER

As a "Story of a Man of Character," *The Mayor of Casterbridge* focuses on how its protagonist's qualities enable him to endure. One tends to think of character, especially in terms of a "Man of Character," as the product of such values as honor and moral righteousness. Certainly Michael Henchard does not fit neatly into such categories. Throughout the novel, his volatile temper forces him into ruthless competition with Farfrae that strips him of his pride and property, while his insecurities lead him to deceive the one person he learns to truly care about, Elizabeth-Jane. Henchard dies an unremarkable death, slinking off to a humble cottage in the woods, and he stipulates in his will that no one mourn or remember him. There will be no statues in the Casterbridge square, as one might imagine, to mark his life and work. Yet Hardy insists that his hero is a worthy man. Henchard's worth, then—that which makes him a "Man of Character"—lies in his determination to suffer and in his ability to endure great pain. He shoulders the burden of his own mistakes as he sells his family, mismanages his business, and bears the storm of an unlucky fate, especially when the furmity-woman confesses and Newson reappears. In a world that seems guided by the "scheme[s] of some sinister intelligence bent on punishing" human beings, there can be no more honorable and more righteous characteristic than Henchard's brand of "defiant endurance."

THE VALUE OF A GOOD NAME

The value of a good name is abundantly clear within the first few chapters of the novel: as Henchard wakes to find that the sale of his wife was not a dream or a drunken hallucination, his first concern is to remember whether he divulged his name to anyone during the course of the previous evening. All the while, Susan warns Elizabeth-Jane of the need for discretion at the Three Mariners Inn—their respectability (and, more important, that of the mayor) could be jeopardized if anyone discovered that Henchard's family performed chores as payment for lodging.

The importance of a solid reputation and character is rather obvious given Henchard's situation, for Henchard has little else besides his name. He arrives in Casterbridge with nothing more than the implements of the hay-trusser's trade, and though we never learn the circumstances of his ascent to civic leader, such a climb presumably depends upon the worth of one's name. Throughout the course of the novel, Henchard attempts to earn, or to believe that he has earned, his position. He is, however, plagued by a conviction of his own worthlessness, and he places himself in situations that can only result in failure. For instance, he indulges in petty jealousy of Farfrae, which leads to a drawn-out competition in which Henchard loses his position as mayor, his business, and the women he loves. More crucial, Henchard's actions result in the loss of his name and his reputation as a worthy and honorable citizen. Once he has lost these essentials, he follows the same course toward death as Lucetta, whose demise is seemingly precipitated by the irretrievable loss of respectability brought about by the "skimmity-ride."

THE INDELIBILITY OF THE PAST

The Mayor of Casterbridge is a novel haunted by the past. Henchard's fateful decision to sell his wife and child at Weydon-Priors continues to shape his life eighteen years later, while the town itself rests upon its former incarnation: every farmer who tills a field turns up the remains of long-dead Roman soldiers. The Ring, the ancient Roman amphitheater that dominates Casterbridge and provides a forum for the secret meetings of its citizens, stands as a potent symbol of the indelibility of a past that cannot be escaped. The terrible events that once occurred here as entertainment for the citizens of Casterbridge have, in a certain sense, determined the town's present state. The brutality of public executions has given way to the miseries of thwarted lovers.

Henchard's past proves no less indomitable. Indeed, he spends the entirety of the novel attempting to right the wrongs of long ago. He succeeds only in making more grievous mistakes, but he never fails to acknowledge that the past cannot be buried or denied. Only Lucetta is guilty of such folly. She dismisses her history with Henchard and the promises that she made to him in order to pursue Farfrae, a decision for which she pays with her reputation and, eventually, her life.

MOTIFS

> *Motifs are recurring structures, contrasts, or literary devices that can help to develop and inform the text's major themes.*

COINCIDENCE

Even the most cursory reading of *The Mayor of Casterbridge* reveals a structural pattern that relies heavily on coincidence. Indeed, the story would hardly progress were it not for the chance occurrences that push Henchard closer and closer to failure. For example, the reappearance of just one long-lost character would test our willingness to believe, but here we witness the return of Susan, the furmity-woman, and Newson, each of whom brings a dark secret that contributes to Henchard's doom. Although we, as modern readers, are unlikely to excuse such overdetermined plotting, we should attempt to understand it. Hardy's reliance on coincidence relates directly to his philosophy of the world. As a determinist, Hardy believed that human life was shaped not by free will but by such powerful, uncontrollable forces as heredity and God. Henchard rails against such forces throughout the novel, lamenting that the world seems designed to bring about his demise. In such an environment, coincidence seems less like a product of poor plot structure than an inevitable consequence of malicious universal forces.

THE TENSION BETWEEN TRADITION AND INNOVATION

Casterbridge is, at first, a town untouched by modernism. Henchard's government runs the town according to quaintly traditional customs: business is conducted by word of mouth and weather-prophets are consulted regarding crop yields. When Farfrae arrives, he brings with him new and efficient systems for managing the town's grain markets and increasing agricultural production. In this way, Henchard and Farfrae come to represent tradition and innovation, respectively. As such, their struggle can be seen not merely as a competition between a grain merchant and his former protégé but rather as the tension between the desire for and the reluctance to change as one age replaces another.

Hardy reports this succession as though it were inevitable, and the novel, for all its sympathies toward Henchard, is never hostile toward progress. Indeed, we witness and even enjoy the efficacy of Farfrae's accomplishments. Undoubtedly, his day of celebration, his new method for organizing the granary's business, and his determination to introduce modern technologies to Casterbridge are good things. Nevertheless, Hardy reports the passing from one era to the next with a quiet kind of nostalgia. Throughout the novel are traces of a world that once was and will never be again. In the opening pages, as Henchard seeks shelter for his tired family, a peasant laments the loss of the quaint cottages that once characterized the English countryside.

The Tension between Public Life and Private Life

Henchard's fall can be understood in terms of a movement from the public arena into the private one. When Susan and Elizabeth-Jane discover Henchard at the Three Mariners Inn, he is the mayor of Casterbridge and its most successful grain merchant, two positions that place him in the center of public life and civic duty. As his good fortune shifts when his reputation and finances fail, he is forced to relinquish these posts. He becomes increasingly less involved with public life—his ridiculous greeting of the visiting Royal Personage demonstrates how completely he has abandoned this realm—and lives wholly with his private thoughts and obsessions. He moves from "the commercial [to] the romantic," concentrating his energies on his personal and domestic relationships with Farfrae, Lucetta, and Elizabeth-Jane.

Symbols

Symbols are objects, characters, figures, or colors used to represent abstract ideas or concepts.

The Caged Goldfinch

In an act of contrition, Henchard visits Elizabeth-Jane on her wedding day, carrying the gift of a caged goldfinch. He leaves the bird in a corner while he speaks to his stepdaughter and forgets it when she coolly dismisses him. Days later, a maid discovers the starved bird, which prompts Elizabeth-Jane to search for Henchard, whom she finds dead in Abel Whittle's cottage. When Whittle reports that Henchard "didn't gain strength, for you see, ma'am, he couldn't eat," he unwittingly ties Henchard's fate to the bird's: both lived and died in a prison. The finch's prison was literal, while Henchard's was the inescapable prison of his personality and his past.

The Bull

The bull that chases down Lucetta and Elizabeth-Jane stands as a symbol of the brute forces that threaten human life. Malignant, deadly, and bent on destruction, it seems to incarnate the unnamed forces that Henchard often bemoans. The bull's rampage provides Henchard with an opportunity to display his strength and courage, thus making him more sympathetic in our eyes.

The Collision of the Wagons

When a wagon owned by Henchard collides with a wagon owned by Farfrae on the street outside of High-Place Hall, the interaction bears more significance than a simple traffic accident. The violent collision dramatically symbolizes the tension in the relationship between the two men. It also symbolizes the clash between tradition, which Henchard embodies, and the new modern era, which Farfrae personifies.

Summary & Analysis

Chapters I–II

In presence of this scene after the other there was a
natural instinct to abjure man as the blot on an
otherwise kindly universe. . . .

(See QUOTATIONS, p. 55)

SUMMARY: CHAPTER I

In the first half of the nineteenth century, a young hay-trusser named Michael Henchard, his wife, Susan, and their baby daughter, Elizabeth-Jane, silently walk along a road in the English countryside toward a large village called Weydon-Priors. They meet a turnip-hoer, and Henchard asks if there is work or shelter to be found in the town. The pessimistic laborer tells the young man that there is neither. The family eventually comes upon a fair and stops for food. They enter a furmity tent, where a woman sells a kind of gruel made from corn, flour, milk, raisins, currants and other ingredients. After watching the woman spike several bowls of the porridge with rum, Henchard slyly sends up his bowl to be spiked as well. The woman accommodates him again and again, and soon Henchard is drunk. As he continues to drink, he bemoans his lot as a married man. If only he were "a free man," he tells the group gathered in the furmity tent, he would "be worth a thousand pound." When the sound of an auctioneer selling horses interrupts Henchard's musings, he jokes that he would be willing to sell his wife if someone wanted to buy her. Susan begs him to stop his teasing, declaring that "this is getting serious. O!—too serious!" Henchard persists nevertheless. He begins to bark out prices like an auctioneer, upping the cost of his wife and child when no one takes his offer. When the price reaches five guineas, a sailor appears and agrees to the trade. Distraught, but glad to leave her husband, Susan go off with Elizabeth-Jane and the sailor. Henchard collapses for the night in the furmity tent.

SUMMARY: CHAPTER II

Henchard wakes the next morning, wondering if the events of the previous night have been a dream. When he finds the sailor's money in his pocket, however, he realizes that he has, in fact, sold his wife and child. He deliberates over his situation for some time and decides that he must "get out of this as soon as [he] can." He exits the tent and makes his way unnoticed from the Weydon fairgrounds. After a mile or so of walking, he stops and wonders if he told his name to anyone at the fair. He is surprised that Susan agreed to go with the sailor and curses her for bringing him "into this disgrace." Still, he resolves to find Susan and Elizabeth-Jane and bear the shame, which he reasons is "of his own making."

Henchard continues on his way, and, three or four miles later, he comes upon a village and enters a church there. He falls to his knees on the altar, places a hand on the Bible, and pledges not to drink alcohol for twenty-one years, the same number of years that he has been alive. He continues the search for Susan and Elizabeth-Jane for several months and eventually arrives at a seaport where a family fitting the description of the sailor, Susan, and Elizabeth-Jane has recently departed. He decides to abandon his search and makes his way to the town of Casterbridge.

ANALYSIS: CHAPTERS I–II

Many critics believe that Michael Henchard, the "Man of Character" to whom the subtitle of *The Mayor of Casterbridge* refers, is one of Thomas Hardy's greatest creations. Henchard is constructed with a great deal of ethical and psychological complexity, and the first two chapters show some of the contradictions of his character. As a young man, Henchard is volatile, headstrong, and passionate. Even before Henchard works himself into a fury in the furmity tent, Susan's meek behavior as she walks along beside him ("she kept as close to his side as was possible without actual contact") implies his volatile and potentially violent nature. The events that take place in the furmity tent at the fair demonstrate a cycle into which Henchard falls frequently throughout the novel. After finding himself in a shameful situation—this time, having sold his wife and child—he takes full responsibility for his mistakes and sets out to correct them. In fact, his desire to make amends is overpowering. He spends several months searching for his wife and child, proving that his remorse is not halfhearted. This audacious spirit is a hallmark of Henchard's character, as he switches quickly from ungrateful misogyny to sincere penitence. Ultimately, though, critics have remained interested in Henchard because his success in atoning for his transgressions is ambiguous.

Although Henchard's search for his wife seems to be an example of honest contrition, his true motivation is more likely concern over his personal honor. When Henchard wakes, his remorse stems more from a fear of being disdained than from any sense of moral irresponsibility. His interest in his good name plays a significant role in his sacrifice of personal satisfaction when he swears off alcohol and determines to find his wife. Before he begins to scour the English countryside for his wife and child, he reflects that it is not his own but rather his wife's "idiotic simplicity" that has brought disgrace on him. As he stands outside the fairgrounds at Weydon-Priors, anxiously wondering whether he revealed his name to anybody in the furmity tent, Henchard displays an obsession with public opinion concerning his character that greatly shapes his actions and personality. Critic Irving Howe refers to this trait as Henchard's "compulsive and self-lacerating pride." Henchard's initial irresponsibility suggests that the novel's subtitle may not be an accurate description of him. In a way, then, the subtitle foreshadows Henchard's transition to a man of character.

Though Hardy resented being labeled a pessimist, the *The Mayor of Casterbridge* is at times bleakly realistic. Hardy described himself as a *meliorist*—one who believes that the universe tends toward improvement and that human beings can enjoy this progress as long as they recognize their proper place in the natural order of things—but the world that the novel describes seems pessimistic and difficult. Hardy uses Susan Henchard, who has "the hard, half-apathetic expression of one who deems anything possible at the hands of Time and Chance except, perhaps, fair play," to demonstrate the importance of realistically understanding the natural order of things. We get the sense that the natural world, embodied by "Time and Chance," has little interest in human life or misery. Hardy substantiates this idea by inserting an image of several horses lovingly rubbing their necks together after the ridiculous scene in the furmity tent. Juxtaposing compassion and heartlessness, Hardy shows us that love and violence are competing aspects of both human behavior and the natural world.

CHAPTERS III–VI

SUMMARY: CHAPTER III

Eighteen years have passed. Two women, Susan Henchard, dressed in the mourning clothes of a widow, and her now-grown daughter, Elizabeth-Jane, walk along the same stretch of road toward Weydon-Priors. As the two make their way toward the fairgrounds, they speak of the sailor, Newson, whom Elizabeth-Jane believes to be her father, and his recent death at sea. Susan explains that they are there to look for a long-lost relative by the name of Henchard. Once at the fair, Susan recognizes the furmity tent and its proprietress, and she takes a private moment to ask the woman whether she remembers a husband selling his wife. After a moment, the furmity-seller does remember, and she states that the man guilty of that deed came back to her tent a year later to ask her to send anyone who came looking for him to the town of Caster-bridge. Susan thanks the woman and sets off with Elizabeth-Jane for Casterbridge.

SUMMARY: CHAPTER IV

As they approach Casterbridge, Susan and Elizabeth-Jane pass by two men who, they believe, mention the name Henchard in their conversation. Elizabeth-Jane asks her mother if she should run after the men to ask them about their relative, but Susan, fearing that Henchard may be a disreputable citizen, advises against it. They arrive in Casterbridge, hungry from their journey, and ask a woman where the nearest baker's shop is. The woman tells them there is no good bread in Casterbridge because the corn-factor has sold "grown wheat," grain that has sprouted before harvest, to the millers and bakers. Susan and Elizabeth-Jane find some biscuits at a nearby shop and head off toward the sound of music in the distance.

SUMMARY: CHAPTER V

Susan and Elizabeth-Jane arrive in front of the King's Arms Inn, where a crowd is gathered before large, open windows. When Elizabeth-Jane asks an old man what is going on, he tells her that there is an important dinner taking place and that Mr. Henchard, who is the mayor of Casterbridge, and other prominent gentlemen of the community are attending. Susan and Elizabeth-Jane are greatly surprised to hear that Henchard is the mayor, and Susan is unsure whether to make her presence known. As the two watch the diners eat, Elizabeth-Jane notices that Henchard's wineglass is never filled, and the old man tells her that the mayor has sworn an oath to abstain from all liquor.

As Susan, Elizabeth-Jane, and the other bystanders watch the proceedings, someone calls out to the mayor to explain the current bread crisis. Henchard assures the crowd that the damaged wheat was not his fault and that he has hired a manager to ensure that the same situation does not happen again. "If anybody will tell me how to turn grown wheat into wholesome wheat," he tells the crowd, "I'll take it back with pleasure. But it can't be done."

SUMMARY: CHAPTER VI

A young Scotchman who happens to be passing by hears the discussion about the wheat. He writes a note and asks a waiter to deliver it to the mayor. The stranger then makes his way to the Three Mariners Inn. Having witnessed this interaction, Elizabeth-Jane is intrigued by the stranger. She and Susan are also looking for a place to stay, so they decide to follow the young man to the Three Mariners Inn. The note is delivered to Henchard, who reads it and seems quite interested. Privately, he asks the waiter about the origin of the note. Upon learning that it came from a young man who has gone to spend the night at the Three Mariners, Henchard also makes his way to the inn.

ANALYSIS: CHAPTERS III–VI

Compared to the high and often unbelievable drama of later chapters, little happens in Chapters III through VI. Given that eighteen years have passed since Henchard's sale of his family at the fair in Weydon-Priors, the function of these chapters is largely expository, and they serve mainly to provide necessary information rather than dramatic development. Here, we learn that Henchard, whose prospects for the future seem limited (if not doomed) after his shameful introduction, has managed to become one of Casterbridge's most prominent citizens. Interestingly, Hardy chooses to bypass the story of Henchard's rise from a young, emotionally volatile hay-trusser to the mayor and primary grain distributor of a small agricultural town. Susan and Elizabeth-Jane's ignorance of Henchard's rise to power emphasizes Hardy's decision to eliminate the story of Henchard's development from the narrative scope of the novel.

Instead, as the full title of the novel promises, the subject of Hardy's focus and interest is Henchard's character. The word "character" has several relevant meanings here. First, and perhaps most obvious, the word connotes the artistic portrayal of a person in a work of fiction. Second, it refers to a quality or feature that distinguishes one person or group from another. In his portrayals of Henchard, Farfrae (the Scotchman), Lucetta, and Elizabeth-Jane, Hardy relies heavily on traits that make his characters subject to larger social phenomena or forces. In these chapters, for example, he establishes the essential conflict between a world marked by tradition—as represented by Henchard, who has no means of salvaging a damaged harvest—and a world marked by progressive and sometimes miraculous modern methods. The third meaning of "character" is the suggestion of moral or ethical strength, as in the novel's subtitle: *A Story of a Man of Character.* Although the narrative traces Henchard's fall from grace and social respectability, it positions him, time and again, as a man of moral integrity through his limitless resolve.

The idea of integrity manifests itself several times during the short dinner at the King's Arms. First, as Elizabeth-Jane notices, Henchard's is the only wineglass among the celebrants' to remain empty. This simple detail balances the image of Henchard, for although he is a man whose temper can lead him to make rash decisions that are as unwise as they are unkind, he is also a man of exceptional resolve and a man who honors the vows—no matter how extreme—that he makes. The incident involving the sale of "grown wheat" offers a look into another of Henchard's interesting motives. A frustrated citizen's questioning of Henchard as to how he plans to repay the villagers for the past points to Henchard's biggest anxiety: how to make amends for past wrongs. Henchard's actions indicate that he wonders if the mistakes of the past can be undone, and he hones his resolve for the possibility that he may be able to atone for it. But, stricken by guilt, first by his sale of his wife and daughter and, eighteen years later, by the suggestion of shady business dealings, Henchard longs to expunge the dark spots from his personal history.

CHAPTERS VII–X

SUMMARY: CHAPTER VII

Susan and Elizabeth-Jane arrive at the Three Mariners Inn and take a room. Fearing that the accommodations are too expensive, Elizabeth-Jane persuades the landlady to allow her to work in exchange for a more affordable rate. The landlady asks her to bring the Scotch gentleman his supper. After completing her chores, Elizabeth-Jane takes a tray of food to Susan. She finds Susan eavesdropping on a conversation in the adjacent room, which is occupied by the Scotchman. The mayor, Susan reports, is conversing with the young Scotchman. The women hear Henchard ask the young man if he is Joshua Jopp, who replied to his advertisement for a corn-factor's manager. The Scotchman announces that his name is Donald Farfrae and that, while he too is in the corn trade, he would not have replied to the advertisement because he is on his way to America. He then demonstrates to Henchard the method for restoring grown wheat described in his note. When Henchard offers to pay him for this information, Farfrae refuses. Henchard offers him the position of manager of the corn branch of his business, but Farfrae declines, intent on traveling to America. Farfrae invites Henchard to have a drink with him, but Henchard confesses his vow to avoid alcohol because of a shameful incident in his past.

SUMMARY: CHAPTER VIII

After Henchard leaves, Farfrae rings for service, and Elizabeth-Jane goes to take away his dinner tray. Once downstairs, she pauses to listen to the musical entertainment. Soon, Farfrae joins the guests and wins them over by singing a song about his homeland. When they learn that Farfrae is just passing through Casterbridge, they express their sorrow over losing such a skilled singer. Watching from the background, Elizabeth-Jane thinks to herself that she and Farfrae are very similar. She decides that they both view life as essentially tragic. As Farfrae prepares to retire to bed, the landlady asks Elizabeth-Jane to go to his room and turn down his bed. Having completed this task, she passes Farfrae on the stairs, and he smiles at her. Meanwhile, Henchard reflects on his fondness for his new acquaintance, thinking that he would have offered Farfrae "a third share in the business to have stayed."

SUMMARY: CHAPTER IX

The next morning, Elizabeth-Jane opens her windows to find Henchard talking to Farfrae. Farfrae tells Henchard that he is about to leave, and they decide to walk together to the edge of town. Susan decides to send Elizabeth-Jane to Henchard with a message. Upon arriving at Henchard's house, Elizabeth-Jane is surprised to find Farfrae in Henchard's office. The narrator explains that when the two men reached the edge of town, Henchard persuaded Farfrae to stay on and work for him, telling the young man that he could name his own terms.

SUMMARY: CHAPTER X

While Elizabeth-Jane waits to speak with Henchard, she overhears a conversation in which Joshua Jopp arrives to accept the position of manager. Henchard tells Jopp that the post has already been filled, and Jopp goes away disappointed. When Elizabeth-Jane finally meets Henchard, she delivers the simple message that his relative, Susan, a sailor's widow, is in town. Upon hearing this news, Henchard ushers her into his dining room and asks her some questions about her mother. He then writes a note to Susan telling her to meet him later that night, encloses five guineas, and gives it to Elizabeth-Jane for delivery. She brings the note back to Susan, who decides to meet Henchard alone.

ANALYSIS: CHAPTERS VII–X

The placement of rural, agricultural Casterbridge on the border between manufacturing and agricultural life makes it the ideal setting for a showdown between Michael Henchard and Donald Farfrae. Even though their relationship is, at this point in the novel, marked by strong mutual affection, Hardy plants the seeds of their eventual competition in these early chapters. When, in Chapter VII, Farfrae claims that he has "some inventions useful to the trade, and there is no scope for developing them here," he suggests that Casterbrige is not only a town straddling the divide between city and country life but also between orthodoxy and modernity or tradition and progress.

Casterbridge under Henchard's reign is too remote and too removed from the scientific, social, and technological advancements that were sweeping through England during Industrial Revolution in the mid-nineteenth century to offer Farfrae the "scope" he seeks. Indeed, before Farfrae arrives, no one in Casterbridge had ever heard of—let alone developed and perfected—a method of restoring "grown wheat." Farfrae brings with him new methods of organizing and running an agricultural business. His dazzling abilities—there is the suggestion of something miraculous in his knowledge of how to transform damaged grain into palatable bread—work their magic on Henchard and, later, the entire town. But the degree to which Henchard is seized by admiration has more to do with the nature of his own character than the quality of Farfrae's impressive and obscure knowledge. What may initially attract Henchard to Farfrae's methods is the promise of transforming something clearly damaged into salvageable goods, a process that Henchard hopes to apply to his own life in order to atone for his sins.

As is evident in the opening scene in which he auctions off his family, Henchard is ruled primarily by his passions. His actions follow from his emotions rather than from his reason or intellect, as when, after Farfrae shares the secret for restoring damaged grain, Henchard offers him a job. Such an action, in itself, may not necessarily seem odd, but Henchard's admiration for Farfrae and his determination to secure his employment seem irrational. It hardly seems prudent for a respected grain merchant to be willing to give away one-third of his business to a man he hardly knows.

If Farfrae represents Henchard's opposite in relation to progress, he also embodies the flip side of the mayor's passion. Farfrae emerges as an emotionally conservative man. Although he proves a kind and attentive listener to the many troubles of Henchard's heart, he never imagines Henchard to be his confidant. Hardy does not suggest that Farfrae is without sin or troubles but, rather, that he approaches them from a more pragmatic perspective. For example, in Chapter VII, Farfrae sings a moving and sentimental tribute to the homeland he has left behind. Even though he feels intense nostalgia for his homeland, he approaches that emotion pragmatically, at the same time understanding his motivations for leaving Scotland behind. In this way, Hardy draws a dividing line between the two men. Whereas Henchard stands for tradition and unfettered emotions, Farfrae embodies progress and reason.

In these chapters, Hardy uses present-tense narration to suggest that the narration is happening at the same time as the events it describes, a style of writing that hearkens back to eighteenth-century novels, such as Henry Fielding's *Tom Jones* and Laurence

Sterne's *Tristram Shandy*. Hardy lends his narrative more immedi-acy—"While Elizabeth-Jane sits waiting in great amaze at the young man's presence we may briefly explain how he came there"—and we get the sense that we are participating in the action and that the events being described are not part of some distant past.

CHAPTERS XI–XIV

SUMMARY: CHAPTER XI
Susan meets Henchard in the Ring, "one of the finest Roman Amphi-theatres, if not the very finest, remaining in Britain." Henchard's first words to Susan are to assure her that he no longer drinks. He asks why she has not returned before now, and she replies that, since she believed the terms of her sale to be binding, she felt unable to leave Newson until his death. They agree that it is impossible for them to begin living together as though they were still married because of Henchard's estimable position in the town, as well as Elizabeth-Jane's ignorance of their dishonorable past. Henchard insists that they proceed with caution and devises a plan: Susan will take a cot-tage in town as the Widow Newson and allow Henchard to court and marry her, thereby restoring both their marriage and his role as Eliz-abeth-Jane's father without revealing their past.

SUMMARY: CHAPTER XII
When Henchard returns home, he encounters Farfrae still at work. He asks Farfrae to leave off working and join him for supper. As the two men eat, Henchard confides in Farfrae about his present situa-tion. He discloses his relationship with Susan, and Farfrae replies that the only solution is to make amends by living with her as hus-band and wife. Henchard reveals that he has become involved with another woman in Jersey, where he once traveled on business. He adds that their affair caused quite a scandal in Jersey, for which the woman suffered greatly. To make amends, Henchard proposed to her, on the condition that she run the risk of his first wife being alive. The woman accepted, but now that Susan has returned he regrets that he will have to disappoint the woman in Jersey. Farfrae assures him that the situation cannot be helped and offers to help Henchard write a letter breaking off relations with the Jersey woman.

SUMMARY: CHAPTER XIII

Susan gets established in a cottage in the town, and Henchard begins to visit her "with business-like determination." Rumors go around the town concerning the two of them, and a wedding soon follows.

SUMMARY: CHAPTER XIV

After Susan and Elizabeth-Jane move in with Henchard, Elizabeth-Jane enjoys a peace of mind that makes her more beautiful. One day, Henchard comments that it is odd that Elizabeth-Jane's hair has lightened since she was a baby. Susan, with "an uneasy expression" on her face, assures him that nothing is amiss. Henchard says he wants to have Elizabeth-Jane's surname legally changed from Newson to Henchard, since she is actually his daughter. Susan proposes the change to Elizabeth-Jane, who, though reluctant, says she will consider it. When, later that day, Elizabeth-Jane asks Henchard if he wishes the change very much, Henchard says it is her decision. The matter is dropped, and Elizabeth-Jane remains Miss Newson.

Meanwhile, Henchard's corn and hay business thrives under Farfrae's management, and the two men become good friends. Elizabeth-Jane notices that, when she and Susan are out walking, Farfrae often looks at them "with a curious interest." One day, Elizabeth-Jane receives a note asking her to come to a granary on a farm at which Henchard has been doing business. Thinking it has something to do with Henchard's business, Elizabeth-Jane goes to the farm but finds no one there. Eventually, Farfrae arrives. When he reveals a note similar to Elizabeth-Jane's, they discover that neither of them wrote to the other. Farfrae theorizes that someone who wished to see them both must have been penned the notes, and so they wait a little longer. They eventually decide that this individual is not coming, and they go home.

ANALYSIS: CHAPTERS XI–XIV

As the Industrial Revolution swept through the English country-side, Hardy witnessed dramatic changes. Isolated agricultural towns like Hardy's native Dorchester, which serves as a model for the fictional Casterbridge, were immutably changed by advances in science and technology. Thus, Hardy's observations of the town's unique topography and customs—the thatched-roof cottages, the Ring, the skimmington ride described in Chapter XXXIX—become a means of preserving a dying culture. Hardy's description of the Ring also serves a thematic purpose, in which the history of the arena supports and confirms the novel's undeniably bleak world-view of the inevitability of human suffering. Having served as a gallows for gruesome public executions, as well as the site of countless "pugilistic encounters," the Ring casts a foreboding shadow over Henchard's meeting with his former wife. But the Ring also stands as a remnant of a culture that no longer exists, which, perhaps, foreshadows Casterbridge's imminent move forward into a more technological future.

Hardy uses foreshadowing liberally throughout *The Mayor of Casterbridge*. A prime example occurs in Chapter XIV, when Susan and Henchard discuss the color of Elizabeth-Jane's hair. Henchard's insistence that Elizabeth-Jane's hair has lightened does as much to signal Elizabeth-Jane's dubious paternity as Susan's nervous reaction to Henchard's insistence ("She looked startled, jerked her foot warningly"). Furthermore, the narrator comments that, when Henchard presses the point, "the same uneasy expression . . . to which the future held the key" appears on Elizabeth-Jane's face. These details gradually begin to indicate that Henchard should question his relationship to Elizabeth-Jane. Here, Hardy's technique draws on the traditions of the Victorian novel, which tended to favor elaborately constructed plots and were often published in serial installments. *The Mayor of Casterbridge* was first published in weekly installments in *Graphic* and *Harper's Weekly* magazines. This mode of publishing presented authors with the challenge of enticing their readers to follow the story and purchase its balance in subsequent issues. Foreshadowing was a favored authorial technique used to keep readers intrigued.

This section also introduces us to Lucetta Templeman. Although she remains unnamed—in these chapters she is merely the woman from Jersey—her presence, in the form of Henchard's confidence to Farfrae, introduces one of the novel's dominant themes, the value of a good name. Lucetta is a woman whose name and reputation have been ruined by her relationship to Henchard. She has suffered scandal because, in Henchard's estimation, "she was terribly careless of appearances." In other words, she has shown little respect for the social conventions that deemed her behavior inappropriate.

Lucetta's inattention to her good name contrasts with the care that the Henchards take in their reputations. When Susan and Elizabeth-Jane arrive in town, for example, Susan regrets allowing her daughter to do chores to pay for their room, because she wants to maintain an air of respectability. Similarly, Henchard's motivations often hinge upon his desire to maintain a respectable appearance and to keep his name in good social standing. Henchard's desire, at the end of Chapter XII, to "make amends to Susan," stems less from a sense of guilt or horror at his past actions than from the need to keep his positions of mayor, churchwarden, and father to Elizabeth-Jane free from "disgrace."

CHAPTERS XV–XVIII

> [T]hey laid a slippery pole, with a live pig . . . tied at the other end, to become the property of the man who could walk over and get it. (See QUOTATIONS, p. 56)

SUMMARY: CHAPTER XV

Henchard and Farfrae have a quarrel over the treatment of Abel Whittle, a man who is consistently late for his job in Henchard's hay-yard. When Whittle is late for work the day after Henchard reprimands him for his tardiness, Henchard goes to his house, drags him out of bed, and sends him to work without his breeches. When Farfrae sees Whittle, who claims that he will later kill himself rather than bear this humiliation, he tells him to go home and dress properly. Henchard and Farfrae confront each other, and Farfrae threatens to leave. The two men reconcile, but Henchard, upset by Farfrae's insubordination, thinks on him with "dim dread" and regrets having "confided to him the secrets of his life."

SUMMARY: CHAPTER XVI

A festival day in celebration of a national event is suggested to the country at large, but Casterbridge is slow to make plans. One day, Farfrae asks Henchard if he can borrow some waterproof cloths to organize a celebration. Henchard tells him he can have as many cloths as he wants. Henchard is inspired to plan events for the holiday and begins to organize a grand entertainment on an elevated green close to the town. When the day of the festival arrives, the weather is overcast, and it rains by midday. Henchard's celebration is ruined, but Farfrae's, which takes place under a tent he has ingeniously constructed, goes off without a hitch. Henchard sees Farfrae at the center of a great ball, dancing with Elizabeth-Jane. Prominent townspeople tease Henchard, remarking that Farfrae will soon surpass his master. Henchard replies that no such thing will happen, stating that Farfrae will shortly be leaving the business.

SUMMARY: CHAPTER XVII

Elizabeth-Jane regrets that she has upset Henchard by dancing with Farfrae. She leaves the tent and stands thinking. After a short time, Farfrae joins her to say that, were circumstances different, he would have asked her something that night. He tells her that he is thinking of leaving Casterbridge, and she says that she wishes he would stay. Later, she is relieved to hear that Farfrae has purchased a small corn and hay business of his own in Casterbridge. Upset by what he takes to be Farfrae's coup, Henchard requests that Elizabeth-Jane break all ties with Farfrae and sends a letter to Farfrae asking the same from him. Elizabeth-Jane dutifully obeys Henchard and engages in no further contact with Farfrae. As Farfrae's new business grows, Henchard becomes increasingly embittered.

SUMMARY: CHAPTER XVIII

Susan falls ill. Henchard receives a letter from Lucetta Templeman, the woman from Jersey with whom he was having an affair. In it she says that she honors his decision to remarry his first wife and understands the impossibility of any further communication between them. She also requests that he return to her the love letters she has written him. She suggests that he do her this favor in person and announces that she will be on a coach passing through Casterbridge. Henchard goes to meet the coach, but Lucetta is not there.

Meanwhile, Susan has gotten worse. One night, she asks Elizabeth-Jane to bring her a pen and paper. She writes a letter, which she seals and marks, "Mr. Michael Henchard. Not to be opened till Elizabeth-Jane's wedding-day." Susan also admits to Elizabeth-Jane that it was she who wrote the notes that caused Elizabeth-Jane and Farfrae to meet at the farm, hoping that the two would fall in love and marry.

Soon thereafter, Susan dies. Farfrae hears some of the old inhabitants of the village discussing her death. One villager, Mother Cuxsom, relates that Susan had laid out all the necessary preparations for her burial, including four pennies for weighing down her eyes. After Susan is buried, Christopher Coney, a poor townsman, digs up her body to retrieve the pennies, arguing that death should not rob life of fourpence.

Farfrae's character was just the reverse of Henchard's,
who might not inaptly be described as Faust has been
described. . . . (See QUOTATIONS, p. 57)

ANALYSIS: CHAPTERS XV–XVIII

If there is a main argument in *The Mayor of Casterbridge*, Hardy states it implicitly in Chapter XVII, where he suggests that "[c]haracter is Fate." These chapters do much to support the notion that one's personality determines the course of one's life—they contain a turning point that hinges upon Henchard's disposition. It is clear that Henchard's emotions dominate his life and tend to determine his actions. When he enters into his friendship with Farfrae, for instance, he does so wholeheartedly. It is not until their relationship begins to sour—first as a result of their disagreement over Abel Whittle and later as a result of Henchard's failed celebration—that Henchard's emotional involvement with and dedication to a man he hardly knows seems reckless. This characteristic extremity of emotion shapes the course of Henchard's life. Just as his exceptional guilt over mistreating Susan leads him to marry for the second time a woman he does not love, his jealousy of Farfrae forces him into a competition that he cannot win.

In terms of their emotional vulnerability, both Elizabeth-Jane and Farfrae stand as counterpoints to Henchard. Their reactions to Henchard's request that they no longer see one another mark them as beings ruled by something other than feeling. Given their mutual affection, their willingness to agree to Henchard's demand without so much as a word of protest seems odd. Of course, it is possible that Farfrae's respect for Henchard's wishes makes him noble (later, while remembering Henchard's initial kindness toward him, Farfrae refers to his loyalty to Henchard). But Farfrae's behavior also reveals his distance from passionate emotion. Similarly, Elizabeth-Jane emerges as a study in emotional moderation. Like Farfrae, she bows to Henchard's wish without objection. Hardy encapsulates her character brilliantly in the opening passage of Chapter XV, in which she carefully constructs an outfit so as not to appear too artful or excessive. Her behavior here serves as an important contrast to that of Lucetta, whose eventual ostentatious appearance matches the excess of her emotions.

The closing scene of Chapter XVIII makes use of a secondary cast of characters that appears throughout the novel. These characters resemble and serve a function similar to that of Shakespeare's rustics in *A Midsummer Night's Dream*—the band of crude, uneducated peasants charged with the responsibility of providing comic relief. With their colorful dialect, the crew of Nance Mockridge and Christopher Coney certainly do lighten the tone of Hardy's tragedy, but the peasants also serve as a Greek chorus, in that they appear on the scene to judge the action of the primary characters and comment on the world at large. Although Christopher Coney's insistence that death should not rob life of four pennies is comical, it also points to the vast and profound nature of human suffering as reflected in these minor characters' poverty and drive to steal.

CHAPTERS XIX–XXII

SUMMARY: CHAPTER XIX
One night, about three weeks after Susan's death, Henchard decides to tell Elizabeth-Jane the truth about the relationship between him and her mother. Henchard does not admit that he sold the pair, but he does tell Elizabeth-Jane that he is her father and that, during Elizabeth-Jane's childhood, he and her mother each thought the other dead.

Henchard asks Elizabeth-Jane to draw up a paragraph for the newspaper announcing that she will change her name to Henchard and then leaves her alone to collect her thoughts. He goes upstairs to search for some documents to prove his relationship to Elizabeth-Jane and discovers the letter that Susan wrote before her death. Despite the request to leave the letter unread until Elizabeth-Jane's wedding-day, Henchard opens it and learns that Elizabeth-Jane is not, in fact, his daughter. The letter informs him that his child died shortly after he and his family parted ways and that the young woman he has welcomed into his home is actually the daughter of the sailor who purchased Susan at Weydon-Priors.

In the morning, Elizabeth-Jane comes to Henchard and tells him that she now intends to look upon him as her true father. Henchard's discovery of the night before renders her acceptance of him bittersweet, but he decides not to traumatize Elizabeth-Jane further with this additional surprise.

SUMMARY: CHAPTER XX

Though Elizabeth-Jane continues to live under his roof, Henchard becomes increasingly cold and distant toward her. He criticizes her country dialect, telling her that such language makes her "only fit to carry wash to a pig-trough," and describes her handwriting as unrefined and unwomanly. One afternoon, Henchard reprimands Elizabeth-Jane for bringing Nance Mockridge, one of the workers in his hay-yard, some bread and cheese. When Nance overhears Henchard insult her character, she tells Henchard that Elizabeth-Jane has waited on worse for hire. Elizabeth-Jane confirms that she once worked at the Three Mariners Inn, leaving Henchard shocked and afraid that Elizabeth-Jane has compromised his reputation through her menial labor. One morning, on her way to visit Susan's grave, Elizabeth-Jane sees a well-dressed lady studying Susan's tombstone. Intrigued, Elizabeth-Jane wonders who she is and thinks about her on the way home.

Meanwhile, Henchard's term as mayor is about to end, and he learns that he will not be named one of the town's aldermen. In light of this fact, he becomes even more annoyed that Elizabeth-Jane was once a servant at the Three Mariners Inn. Henchard is further rankled when he learns that she served Donald Farfrae. Considering Elizabeth-Jane a burden of which he would like to rid himself, Henchard writes to Farfrae withdrawing his disapproval of their courtship. The next day, Elizabeth-Jane meets the well-dressed lady in the churchyard. As they talk, Elizabeth-Jane reveals that she is not entirely happy with her father. The lady asks if Elizabeth-Jane will come live with her as a companion, explaining that she is about to move into High-Place Hall, near the center of Casterbridge. Elizabeth-Jane gladly agrees, and the lady arranges to meet her again in a week.

SUMMARY: CHAPTER XXI

During the next week, Elizabeth-Jane walks by High-Place Hall many times and thinks about what it will be like to live there. One day, while looking at the house, she hears someone approaching and hides. Henchard enters the house without noticing or being noticed by Elizabeth-Jane. Later that day, Elizabeth-Jane asks Henchard if he has any objection to her leaving his house. He answers that he has no objections whatsoever and even offers to give her an allowance.

The appointed day for Elizabeth-Jane's meeting with the well-dressed lady arrives, and she goes to the churchyard as planned. The lady is there and introduces herself as Miss Templeman. She tells Elizabeth-Jane that she can join her at High-Place Hall immediately, and Elizabeth-Jane rushes home to pack her things. Watching her, Henchard regrets his treatment of Elizabeth-Jane and asks her to stay. But she cannot, she says, since she is on her way to High-Place Hall, leaving Henchard dumbfounded.

SUMMARY: CHAPTER XXII

The narrator shifts back to the night prior to Elizabeth-Jane's departure, when Henchard receives a letter from Lucetta announcing that she has moved to Casterbridge and will take up residence at High-Place Hall. He then receives another letter, shortly after Elizabeth-Jane leaves, in which Lucetta asks him to call on her. He goes that night but is told that she is busy, though she would be happy to see him the next day. Upset by this rebuff, he resolves not to visit her. The next day, Lucetta waits expectantly for Henchard and is disappointed when he does not come. While she waits, she and Elizabeth-Jane look out on the market and discuss the town and its inhabitants.

Several days pass without a visit from Henchard. Three days later, Lucetta comments to Elizabeth-Jane that Henchard may come to visit her (Elizabeth-Jane). Elizabeth-Jane tells Lucetta that she does not believe he will, because they have quarreled too much. Lucetta then decides to send Elizabeth-Jane on some useless errands and quickly writes a letter to Henchard saying that she has sent Elizabeth-Jane away and asking him to visit. A visitor finally arrives, but when he enters Lucetta sees that he is not Henchard.

ANALYSIS: CHAPTERS XIX–XXII

The presence of several extremely unlikely coincidences in these chapters underscores the fact that *The Mayor of Casterbridge* does not attempt to portray reality. Even before this section of the novel, a number of rather fantastic occurrences have accumulated: not only does Henchard sell his wife and daughter, but Susan happens to come upon the furmity-woman who not only has witnessed the event of eighteen years ago but also remembers that Henchard left for Casterbridge, where he still happens to live.

The many coincidences in Henchard's life serve an important function in that they confirm Hardy's bleak conception of the world. In each of his major novels, Hardy makes his characters suffer in unbearable circumstances and, as a result, learn their true place in the universe. As he begins to lose the comforts and position of mayor and businessman, Henchard moves more steadily toward an understanding of life's harshness. In Chapter XIX, he muses, "I am to suffer, I perceive. This much scourging, then, is it for me?" attempting to understand the reality of his emotional pain. As life presents unpleasant obstacles, Henchard becomes convinced there is "some sinister intelligence bent on punishing" him. His acceptance of suffering—"misery taught him nothing more than defiant endurance of it"—illustrates his bleak and fatalistic outlook. The twists and turns of the novel's plot, each of which serves to tighten the screws on Henchard's misery, derive from Hardy's belief that the universe is designed to create human suffering.

Because this philosophy dominates the novel, *The Mayor of Casterbridge* is a prime example of naturalistic writing. This school of writing, prevalent in the late nineteenth century, sought to render ordinary life. According to the naturalist novelist Frank Norris, it concentrates on "the smaller details of everyday life, things that are likely to happen between lunch and supper." Naturalism describes the details of everyday life but does so according to the philosophical tenets of *determinism,* the belief that human beings are shaped by the forces that operate on them. Certainly these forces—whether they are the workings of fate or social conventions—are the forms of "sinister intelligence" that Henchard believes are bent on punishing him.

Chapters XXIII–XXVI

Summary: Chapter XXIII

Lucetta invites Farfrae, who has come looking for Elizabeth-Jane, to sit down. The two talk and watch the bustling marketplace from Lucetta's window. They witness a farmer negotiating the employment of an old shepherd. The farmer refuses to take the old man if his son is not part of the bargain, but the young man is hesitant to go, for it means leaving behind the girl he loves. Touched by this scene, Farfrae goes out and hires the young man so that he can remain close to his love. Minutes after Farfrae leaves, Henchard

arrives, but Lucetta has her maid tell Henchard that she has a head-
ache and does not wish to see him that day.

SUMMARY: CHAPTER XXIV

Elizabeth-Jane enjoys living with Lucetta, and the days pass pleas-
antly for both. One day, they look out their window at the market and
see the demonstration of a "new-fashioned agricultural implement."
When they go out to take a closer look at it, they meet Henchard, who
ridicules the machine. Elizabeth-Jane introduces him to Lucetta, but
as he turns to leave she thinks she hears him accuse Lucetta of refusing
to see him. Elizabeth-Jane's suspicions are aroused, but she decides
that she must have heard Henchard incorrectly.

Farfrae appears and praises the usefulness of the new machine.
Elizabeth-Jane wonders about Henchard's familiarity with Lucetta
but soon learns that they have met previously and that Lucetta is
interested in Farfrae. One day, Lucetta tells Elizabeth-Jane a story.
Claiming to seek advice for a "friend," she relates her present situation with Henchard and Farfrae. Elizabeth-Jane is not fooled by the
claim that the story is about a friend and tells Lucetta that she cannot give an opinion on such a difficult subject.

SUMMARY: CHAPTER XXV

Farfrae continues to call on Lucetta with increasing frequency. One
day, while Elizabeth-Jane is out, Henchard calls on Lucetta and tells
her that he is ready for them to be married. He claims that he is
doing her a favor by making "an honest proposal for silencing [her]
Jersey enemies," but Lucetta resists. She refuses to be a slave to the
past and defiantly claims, "I'll love where I choose!"

SUMMARY: CHAPTER XXVI

Henchard and Farfrae meet one day while walking, and Henchard
asks the younger man if he recalls the story of the woman from Jersey whom he gave up in order to remarry his first wife. He tells
Farfrae that the Jersey woman now refuses to marry him, and
Farfrae states that Henchard has no further obligation to her. Later,
Henchard visits Lucetta and asks if she knows Farfrae. She says that
she does, but she downplays the significance of her reply by claiming to know almost everyone in Casterbridge. Just then, someone
knocks at the door, and Farfrae enters. Henchard thus begins to sus-
pect that Farfrae is his rival for Lucetta's affections.

Henchard decides to hire Joshua Jopp, the man whose managerial position he had earlier given to Farfrae. He tells Jopp that his primary objective is to cut Farfrae out of the corn and hay business. In order to discern harvest conditions, Henchard consults a man known as a "forecaster" or weather prophet. This man predicts that the harvest will bring rain, so Henchard, trusting that the upcoming crop will be bad, buys a large quantity of corn. When harvest comes, however, the weather is fair and the crop is good, which causes prices to fall. Henchard loses money and fires Joshua Jopp.

ANALYSIS: CHAPTERS XXIII–XXVI

The chapters in this section foretell the transition of a quaint Casterbridge that stands isolated from modern times into a more industrialized, economically viable town. Under Henchard's reign as mayor, the town does not flourish; rather, it merely, like Henchard, endures. Indeed, when the novel opens, the citizens find themselves in dire straits over a damaged crop. Without Farfrae to introduce the modern method by which grown wheat can be restored, one imagines that the people of Casterbridge would have continued to suffer with their hunger and that Henchard would have sought in vain for a way to make amends. But as Henchard falls, so too do the proverbial walls that keep progress and modernity at bay. Hardy uses Henchard's reliance on the outdated weather prophet to encapsulate a fading, bygone era. In the face of progress—embodied by Farfrae in his reliance on and fondness for modern machinery—Henchard cannot compete.

Although the novel proclaims itself, in its subtitle, *A Story of a Man of Character* and, as such, concentrates primarily on Henchard, these chapters provide us with a keener understanding of Farfrae, Elizabeth-Jane, and Lucetta. In many ways, Lucetta Templeman seems familiar. Like Henchard, she is ruled by her passions. Just as she once refused to conceal her affair with Henchard to secure her good name in Jersey, she now refuses to bow to his whims or his threats and marry him against her will. In her declaration that she will love whomever she chooses, we recognize the same sort of blind resolve that possesses and often misleads Henchard.

But Lucetta differs from her ex-lover in a crucial respect: she refuses to enslave herself to the past. She recognizes no obligations, feels no compulsion toward self-sacrifice, and voices no desire to make amends. That Henchard does oblige himself to right past wrongs and so willingly flays himself for his sins sets him apart. Indeed, it is this desire to undo the past, regardless of what it means for his present or future life, that makes Henchard a man of character and proves the rarity and worth of his moral fiber.

While Henchard and Lucetta have similar capacities for emotional vulnerability, Farfrae and Elizabeth-Jane stand as their opposites. Throughout the novel, these two demonstrate a tendency for sentimentality—Farfrae sings sad songs of the homeland he misses, for example, and Elizabeth-Jane pines for Henchard's love and attention—but both are capable of a curious emotional detachment that suggests they are ruled by their heads rather than their hearts. In matters of love, for instance, Farfrae proves himself rather passionless. He resumes courtship of Elizabeth-Jane as quickly and with as little ceremony as he abandons it, which makes his motivation seem more a matter of wise business, such as an alliance with Henchard through marriage, than personal desire. The same might be said of Elizabeth-Jane, who accepts the dawning knowledge of Lucetta's affair with Farfrae, the man she supposedly loves, stoically.

CHAPTERS XXVII–XXX

SUMMARY: CHAPTER XXVII
While corn prices are low, Farfrae buys a large amount of corn, and the weather suddenly turns poor again, causing the harvest to be less successful than predicted. Farfrae prospers as the corn prices rise, and Henchard laments his rival's success. One night, one of Farfrae's wagoners and one of Henchard's collide in the street in front of High-Place Hall. Henchard is summoned to settle the dispute. Lucetta and Elizabeth-Jane testify that Henchard's man was in the wrong, but Henchard's man maintains that these two cannot be trusted because "all the women side with Farfrae."

After the conflict is resolved, Henchard calls on Lucetta and is told that she cannot see him because she has an appointment. He hides outside her door and sees Farfrae call for her. As the couple leave for a walk, Henchard follows them and eavesdrops on their declarations of love. When Lucetta returns to High-Place Hall, Henchard surprises her there. He threatens to reveal their past intimacy unless she agrees to marry him. With Elizabeth-Jane as a witness, she agrees to do so.

Summary: Chapter XXVIII

The next day, Henchard goes to Town Hall to preside over a case (he retains his position as a magistrate for one year after being mayor). There is only one case to be heard—that of an old woman accused of disorderly conduct. The constable testifies that the woman insulted him, and the woman interrupts many times during his testimony with objections. Finally, the woman is granted the opportunity to offer her defense. She recounts the story of an event that happened twenty years ago. She was a furmity-merchant at a fair in Weydon-Priors and witnessed a man sell his wife to a sailor for five guineas. She identifies Henchard as the guilty party and asks how such a man can sit in judgment of her. The clerk dismisses the story as mere fabrication, but Henchard admits its truth and leaves the court. Lucetta sees a crowd around the Town Hall and asks her servant what is happening. The servant tells her of Henchard's revelation, and Lucetta becomes deeply miserable that she has agreed to marry him. She departs to the seaside town of Port-Bredy for a few days.

Summary: Chapter XXIX

Lucetta walks along the road toward Port-Bredy. She stops a mile outside of Casterbridge and sees Elizabeth-Jane, who has decided to meet her, approaching. Suddenly, a bull begins to walk toward them, and the two women retreat into a nearby barn. The bull charges and traps them in the barn. The bull chases them until a man appears; he seizes the bull by its nose ring and secures it outside the barn. The man turns out to be Henchard, and Lucetta is very grateful to him for saving them. The trio heads home. Lucetta remembers that she has dropped her muff in the barn, and Elizabeth-Jane offers to run back and get it. After finding the muff, Elizabeth-Jane runs into Farfrae on the road. He drives her home, then returns to his own lodging, where his servants are preparing to move.

Meanwhile, Henchard escorts Lucetta home, apologizing for his insistence that she marry him. He suggests an indefinite engagement. When she asks if there is anything she can do to repay his kindness, he asks her to tell Mr. Grower, one of his creditors, that they will soon be married—given Lucetta's wealth, Henchard believes that this arrangement will persuade Grower to treat his debt more leniently. Lucetta replies that she cannot do so, since Grower served as a witness during her wedding to Farfrae, which she announces, took place this week secretly in Port-Bredy.

SUMMARY: CHAPTER XXX

Shortly after Lucetta arrives at home, Farfrae follows with all his things. All that remains to be done, she claims, is to tell Elizabeth-Jane of their marriage. Lucetta goes to speak to Elizabeth-Jane and asks if she remembers the story about her friend who was torn between the two lovers. Elizabeth-Jane remembers, and Lucetta makes it clear that that the "friend" of whom she was speaking is actually herself. Lucetta tells Elizabeth-Jane that she wishes her to stay in the house as before, and Elizabeth-Jane says that she will think about it. As soon as Lucetta leaves the room, however, Elizabeth-Jane makes preparations to depart and does so later that night.

ANALYSIS: CHAPTERS XXVII–XXX

The clash between the wagoners of Farfrae and Henchard is symbolic of the larger clash between the two men and the forces they represent. As the drivers meet on the cramped street outside High-Place Hall, the confrontation seems to indicate a clash between two competing corn merchants. But the confrontation is also between age and youth, tradition and modernity, past and future.

The Mayor of Casterbridge is filled with such symbolic events; one of Hardy's preferred techniques is the encapsulation of larger issues and conflicts into passing details. Another example of this technique is Lucetta and Elizabeth-Jane's confrontation with the bull. If malicious forces dominate the world, then the bull might be read as a manifestation of those forces. It tracks Lucetta as deliberately as her past and the scandal that ultimately destroys her. This scene also provides a moving counterpoint to Henchard's decline. Having lost his position of mayor, his prominence as a business-man, and now, with the testimony of the furmity-woman, much of his dignity, Henchard is given the opportunity to demonstrate what he still possesses. His physical strength is on display as he corrals the bull and ushers the women to safety, but so too is the generosity of his spirit. Although he is increasingly estranged from Lucetta and Elizabeth-Jane, he risks danger on their behalf, proving that, despite bouts of petty behavior, he is essentially a good man, in full control and possessing fortitude and resolve.

In this section, Henchard's beneficence becomes clearer through his responsible reaction to the furmity-woman's accusations against him. A man in Henchard's position could easily dismiss the old woman's accusations and protect his reputation. The other aldermen turn to Henchard, expecting he will deny her charges. Henchard's willingness to admit the truth of the furmity-woman's story elevates the former mayor in our eyes: he seems dedicated to the truth, even when the truth threatens disastrous consequences. However, Henchard is not moved to confess by some romantic appreciation of the truth. In fact, Henchard has chosen not to tell the truth numerous times throughout the novel: he makes a pact to keep the past a secret from Elizabeth-Jane, then, upon discovering that he is not her biological father, keeps this information from her as well. Given the degree of guilt Henchard feels after selling Susan and her daughter, we can assume there is a degree of masochism in Henchard's admission in the courtroom: he is still punishing himself for his past misdoings. By this point, his residual guilt and self-inflicted punishments have assumed the force of a habit.

Hardy suggests also that Henchard's self-destructive actions are a result of his overly direct nature, a characteristic he rarely represses in the novel. If Henchard fully believes that "some power was working against him" and that he is destined to fail, then his confession to the aldermen is an acknowledgment of his inevitable fate. His "sledge-hammer directness" may serve him well in the town's court, but it is disastrous in terms of public relations.

CHAPTERS XXXI–XXXIV

SUMMARY: CHAPTER XXXI

The furmity-woman's revelation about Henchard's past spreads through the town, overshadowing all the "amends he had made." His reputation as a man of honor and prosperity declines rapidly. One day, Elizabeth-Jane notices a crowd gathered outside the King's Arms (the inn at which she first sees Henchard presiding over the prestigious dinner as mayor). She learns that the town commissioners are meeting with regard to Henchard's bankruptcy. Having surrendered all his assets, Henchard offers the commission his last valuable possession: a gold watch. Though they find the gesture honorable, the commissioners refuse. Henchard sells the watch himself and offers the money to one of his smaller creditors. When the remainder of Henchard's effects are auctioned off, Farfrae purchases his business. Elizabeth-Jane makes numerous attempts to contact Henchard, wishing for an opportunity to "forgive him for his roughness to her, and to help him in his trouble," but to no avail. Henchard moves into a cottage owned by Joshua Jopp.

SUMMARY: CHAPTER XXXII

In Casterbridge, there are two bridges where "all the failures of the town" congregate. One evening, while Henchard stands on the more remote bridge, Jopp meets him and explains that Lucetta and Farfrae have just moved into Henchard's old house, which Farfrae purchased along with all of Henchard's furniture. Jopp leaves, and Henchard is soon met by another traveler, Farfrae himself. Having heard that Henchard plans to leave Casterbridge, Farfrae proposes that he live in the spare rooms of his old house. Henchard refuses. Farfrae then offers Henchard whatever furniture he might want. Henchard, though moved by the man's generosity, still refuses.

Elizabeth-Jane learns Henchard has fallen ill and uses his confinement as an excuse to see him. At first, Henchard tells her to go away, but she stays and not only nurses him to a quick recovery but provides him with a new outlook on life. Henchard goes to Farfrae's corn-yard to seek employment as a hay-trusser. When he hears that Farfrae is being considered for mayor, however, he begins to lapse into his old moodiness, counting the number of days until his oath to abstain from alcohol is up. When that day arrives, Elizabeth-Jane hears that Henchard has begun to drink again.

SUMMARY: CHAPTER XXXIII

After Sunday church services, the men of Casterbridge gather at the Three Mariners Inn to discuss the sermon, sing, and "limit [themselves] to half-a-pint of liquor." Released from his vow, Henchard flouts this tradition by getting drunk and singing insulting words about Farfrae to the tune of a psalm. Elizabeth-Jane arrives to bring Henchard home. On their way, he complains that Farfrae has taken everything from him and that he will not be responsible for his deeds should they meet. Worried that Henchard will make good on this threat, she decides to keep an eye on him and, during the week, goes to the hay-yard to help him with his work.

Several days later, Farfrae and Lucetta come to the hay-yard. Lucetta is surprised to see Henchard there. Henchard speaks to her with bitter sarcasm, and the next day she sends him a note asking him not to treat her so poorly. With this incident, the gulf between Henchard and Lucetta grows wider. Later, Elizabeth-Jane observes Henchard and Farfrae on the top floor of the corn-stores and believes she sees Henchard extend his arm as if to push Farfrae. She decides it is her duty to warn him of the apparent danger in which he is placing himself by associating with Henchard.

SUMMARY: CHAPTER XXXIV

The next morning, Elizabeth-Jane approaches Farfrae as he leaves his house. She warns him that Henchard may try to harm him. Unable to contemplate such evil motives, Farfrae dismisses the warning. Wanting to provide a "new beginning" for the man who, years earlier, had offered him a job and position, Farfrae arranges to purchase a seed shop that Henchard can manage. While Farfrae and the town clerk arrange the matter, the town clerk confirms that Henchard hates Farfrae. Farfrae is troubled by this news and decides to delay the purchase of the seed shop.

At home, Farfrae laments to Lucetta that Henchard dislikes him. Afraid that he will learn of her former involvement with Henchard, she urges him to move away from Casterbridge. As they discuss this plan, however, one of the town's aldermen comes to their house to inform them that the newly elected mayor has just died. He asks Farfrae if he will accept the position; Farfrae agrees to do so.

Lucetta asks Henchard once again to return her letters. Realizing that the letters are locked in the safe of his old house, Henchard calls on Farfrae one evening to retrieve them and, while there, reads several letters to Farfrae. Farfrae still does not know that Lucetta wrote the letters, and so he listens to Henchard politely but with little interest. Tempted as he is to reveal the author of the correspondence, Henchard cannot bring himself to ruin Farfrae and Lucetta's marriage.

ANALYSIS: CHAPTERS XXXI–XXXIV

After word spreads of the furmity-woman's accusation, it is remarkable how quickly and completely Henchard "passe[s] the ridge of prosperity and honour and [begins] to descend on the other side." Whereas he earlier enjoys a position of prominence as the mayor of the town, he now stands on a bridge where thwarted lovers and other desperate figures contemplate suicide. Henchard's desperation has much to do with Farfrae and his successes, which seem like some sort of betrayal to Henchard, who helped Farfrae establish himself in Casterbridge. Since Farfrae's introduction, he and Henchard have moved steadily in opposite directions, the former toward prosperity and achievement, the latter toward failure and obscurity. In these chapters, where Farfrae purchases the debt-ridden Henchard's home and business, the transition is complete. Whatever bright eminence the former mayor enjoyed is now eclipsed by his protégé's development, as the refurbished sign outside the grain market makes clear: "A smear of decisive lead-coloured paint had been laid on to obliterate Henchard's name, though its letters dimly loomed through like ships in a fog. Over these, in fresh white, spread the name of Farfrae."

We can understand why Henchard would wish not to live with the man he considers his archrival, let alone with his ex-lover, but his refusal of Farfrae's charity is, as these chapters illustrate, more a function of his character than an aspect of his relationship with Farfrae. Henchard does everything to an extreme: he cannot merely be dissatisfied with married life but, instead, must feel the need to sell his wife; he cannot drink responsibly but, instead, must swear off liquor for twenty-one years, only to return to it with an alcoholic's vengeance. Similarly, just as his emotions for Farfrae run hot or cold, his extreme contempt for Elizabeth-Jane becomes a boundless and needy love. The extremity of Henchard's passions is, in large part, responsible for the severity of his fall. Hardy, appropriating the words of the eighteenth-century German writer Novalis, stresses that "[c]haracter is Fate." Henchard's response to his bankruptcy hearing validates such a hypothesis. His extreme emotions and inability to compromise or show restraint lead him to sell his last valuable possession, his gold watch. Thus, an honorable act launches him further into poverty and despair.

Henchard's behavior remains consistent throughout the novel. He does not undergo a significant change, nor does he learn from his past mistakes and alter his ways. Farfrae's plan to purchase a small seed store for Henchard to manage shows that Farfrae does believe that such change is possible. Ultimately, though, the novel adheres to a philosophy of determinism, which suggests that human beings are never free enough to exert their own will on the universe. Instead, there are forces that determine the course of every human life, regardless of human desire. As Henchard observes: "See now how it's ourselves that are ruled by the Powers above us! We plan this, but we do that."

Chapters XXXV–XXXVIII

Summary: Chapter XXXV

Lucetta overhears the conversation between Farfrae and Henchard and becomes extremely agitated, fearing that Henchard will reveal her authorship of the letters. When Farfrae comes upstairs, she gathers that Henchard has not disclosed her. The next morning, she writes to Henchard, arranging a meeting for later that day at the Ring. There, she begs him to have mercy on her and return the letters, which he agrees to do.

Summary: Chapter XXXVI

When Lucetta returns from her meeting with Henchard, she finds Joshua Jopp waiting for her. He has heard that Farfrae is looking for a business partner and asks if she would recommend him. She refuses, and he returns home disappointed. When Jopp gets home, Henchard asks him to deliver a packet to Mrs. Farfrae. Jopp inspects the packet, discovers that it contains letters, and then goes on his way to deliver it.

Jopp meets the peasant women Mother Cuxsom and Nance Mockridge, who tell him they are on their way to Mixen Lane, the center for "much that was sad, much that was low, some things that were baneful" in Casterbridge. Jopp accompanies them and meets the old furmity-woman, who asks about the parcel he carries. He replies that they are love letters and reads them aloud to the crowd. Nance Mockridge exclaims that Lucetta is the author of the letters and remarks that this information provides a good foundation for a "skimmity-ride," a traditional English spectacle the purpose of which was to express public disapproval of adultery. A stranger, dressed in a fur coat and sealskin cap, expresses interest in the custom and donates some money for the ceremony. Jopp returns home, reseals the letters, and delivers them to Lucetta the next morning.

Summary: Chapter XXXVII

The citizens of Casterbridge soon become aware that a "Royal Personage" plans to pass through the town. The town council, which is to address this esteemed guest, meets to arrange the details of the event, and Henchard interrupts the meeting to ask if he can participate. Farfrae says that Henchard's involvement would not be proper, since he is no longer a member of the council. Henchard vows that he will welcome the Royal Personage in his own way. The special day arrives, and, as the royal carriage stops, a drunken Henchard stands in front of it waving a handmade flag. Farfrae forcefully drags Henchard away.

SUMMARY: CHAPTER XXXVIII

Incensed by Farfrae's treatment of him, Henchard decides to seek revenge. He leaves a message at Farfrae's house requesting that Farfrae meet him at the granaries. When Farfrae arrives, Henchard, who has tied one of his arms to make a more even match, tells him that they will finish the fight begun that morning. The men wrestle, and though Henchard overpowers Farfrae, he cannot bring himself to finish off his opponent. Farfrae leaves, and Henchard is flooded with shame and fond memories of Farfrae. He feels the desire to see Farfrae again but remembers hearing that Farfrae was to leave on a journey for the town of Weatherbury.

ANALYSIS: CHAPTERS XXXV–XXXVIII

Because Henchard feels things more deeply than any other character, with such conviction and force, it is difficult to hold him accountable for his actions. When, for example, he reads Lucetta's letters to Farfrae, he does so not to torment the woman who eavesdrops from a neighboring room, but because he is seized by the profound and helpless feeling that he has been wronged. Similarly, his determination to fight Farfrae arises not from the "rivalry, which ruined" him or the "snubbing, which humbled" him, but rather from the "hustling that disgraced" him. Henchard's concern about his public image makes him particularly despise the idea of being disgraced (this same concern compels him to seek to make amends with Susan nearly two decades after their shameful parting). When he fights Farfrae, then, he is motivated less by vengeance than the need to free himself from the burden of feeling shamed. Indeed, Henchard's complete subservience to his own emotions is manifested in his cries as he breaks from the struggle that "no man ever loved another as I did thee at one time. . . . And now—though I came here to kill 'ee, I cannot hurt thee!"

Though powerful, Henchard is no bully, and he uses his both his physical and political strength sparingly. Though he laments that he has taken Farfrae's dismissal "like a lamb," he wants nothing more than a fair fight from the Scotchman. This desire for fairness is further manifested in his decision to bind one arm before the wrestling match begins, since he is the stronger of the two men. Furthermore, he cannot bring himself to destroy Lucetta, whose duplicity and wayward emotions have left him feeling abandoned and unloved. Nothing would be easier for Henchard than to bring shame upon Lucetta, but he determines, quite honorably, that "such a woman was very small deer to hunt." These moments of restraint—rare for a man of Henchard's domineering passions—prove and preserve Henchard's humanity. Indeed, these conflicts reveal the complexity of Henchard's character and are the reason that many critics have found him to be the most human of all Hardy's creations.

In addition to giving us a more fully developed understanding of Henchard's character, these chapters build suspense by hinting at two major imminent events: the skimmity-ride and the arrival of Newson. The interest displayed in the skimmity-ride, manifest in the fur-wearing stranger's piqued curiosity about the ritual, hints at the ride's inevitability. The ride was a custom popular in rural towns and involved a parade of effigies and music used to shame publicly those guilty (or suspected) of adultery. Although the custom was prohibited by law in 1882, it continued for years after. Hardy foreshadows Newson's arrival very cleverly, using the details of his clothes. In describing a stranger "dressed with a certain clumsy richness—his coat being furred, and his head covered with a cap of seal-skin," Hardy evokes the weatherproofed sailor who, as many years ago at Weydon-Priors, has money at his disposal.

CHAPTERS XXXIX–XLII

SUMMARY: CHAPTER XXXIX

The narrator shifts back to the moments following the wrestling match between Henchard and Farfrae. After Farfrae descends from the loft, Abel Whittle delivers a note to Farfrae requesting his presence in Weatherbury. The note has been sent by some of Farfrae's workers who hope to get Farfrae out of town in order to lessen the damaging impact of the "skimmity-ride." After Farfrae departs for Weatherbury, Lucetta hears commotion in the distance. Outside her window, she overhears two maids describe the proceedings: two figures are sitting back to back on a donkey that is being paraded through the streets of Casterbridge. Just as Elizabeth-Jane enters the room and tries to close the shutters, Lucetta realizes that the figures

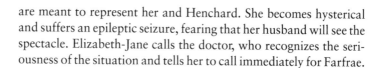

are meant to represent her and Henchard. She becomes hysterical and suffers an epileptic seizure, fearing that her husband will see the spectacle. Elizabeth-Jane calls the doctor, who recognizes the seriousness of the situation and tells her to call immediately for Farfrae.

SUMMARY: CHAPTER XL

Having observed the skimmity-ride, Henchard goes in search of Elizabeth-Jane. Upon arriving at Farfrae's house and learning of Lucetta's condition, Henchard explains that Farfrae must be found on the way to a town called Weatherbury, not another town called Budmouth as originally planned. Because no one believes him, he departs to find Farfrae himself. Eventually, he comes upon Farfrae and urges him to return to Casterbridge, but Farfrae distrusts him and refuses to return. Henchard rides back to Casterbridge only to find that Lucetta is no better. When he returns home, Joshua Jopp tells him that a seaman of some sort called for him while he was out. Farfrae finally returns and sends for another doctor, and Lucetta is much calmed by her husband's arrival. He sits with her through the night as Henchard paces the streets, making inquiries about the patient's health. Early the next morning, a maid informs him that Lucetta is dead.

SUMMARY: CHAPTER XLI

After hearing of of Lucetta's death, Henchard goes home and is soon visited by Elizabeth-Jane. She falls asleep as Henchard prepares her breakfast, and Henchard, not wanting to disturb her, waits patiently for her to wake. Feeling a surge of love for Elizabeth-Jane, he hopes that she will continue to treat him as her father. Just then, a man knocks at the door and introduces himself as Newson. He says that his marriage to Susan had been happy until someone suggested to her that their relationship was a mockery; she then became miserable. Newson adds that he let Susan believe that he was lost at sea. He tells Henchard that he has heard of Susan's death and asks about Elizabeth-Jane. Henchard tells him that the girl is dead as well, and Newson departs in sorrow.

Although it appears that Newson is gone, Henchard remains paranoid that his deception will be discovered and that Newson will return to take Elizabeth-Jane away from him. Elizabeth-Jane wakes, and the two sit down to breakfast. When she leaves, however, he becomes despondent, fearing that she will soon forget him. The rest of his life seems unendurable to him, and he goes to the river just outside of Casterbridge with thoughts of drowning himself. As he prepares to throw himself into the water, he sees his image floating in the pool and desists.

Henchard returns home and finds Elizabeth-Jane waiting outside his door. She says she has come back because he seemed sad that morning. He brings her to the river to show her the image, and she realizes that it must be the effigy from the skimmity-ride. Henchard remarks how strange it is that the performance that killed Lucetta has actually kept him alive. Elizabeth-Jane realizes what he means by this statement and asks if she can come to live with him; he joyfully assents.

SUMMARY: CHAPTER XLII

Henchard continues to fear Newson's return, but, meanwhile, he and Elizabeth-Jane live happily in his home. They see Farfrae only occasionally, as Henchard now owns a small seed and root business that Farfrae and other members of the town council purchased for him. One day, Henchard observes Farfrae looking at Elizabeth-Jane and begins to think of the possibility of their union. He is very much opposed to the idea but decides he should let Elizabeth-Jane make her own decision. As time passes, Elizabeth-Jane and Farfrae begin to meet more frequently. Eventually, Henchard obtains proof of their intimacy when he sees Farfrae kiss Elizabeth-Jane.

ANALYSIS: CHAPTERS XXXIX–XLII

In these chapters, the full complexity of Henchard's character reveals itself. Despite his hatred for someone who now enjoys all the benefits he once did—his business and his lover—he cannot bring himself to enact the vengeance he desires. Instead of seeking revenge, Henchard takes it upon himself to fetch Farfrae and urge him back to Lucetta's bedside. When Henchard declares to Farfrae, "I am a wretched man but my heart is true to you still," his words point not to the fickleness of his affections but to the deeply conflicted nature of his psyche. His motivations are as muddled as his emotions: given his previous efforts to protect his name and reputation, Henchard may hope to mend his damaged image in the eyes of those who "would not believe him, taking his words [regarding Farfrae's whereabouts] but as the frothy utterances of recklessness." But a self-imposed desire to restore his good name is not the only thing that sets Henchard on the road to Weatherbury. As his unwillingness to pummel Farfrae when he has him pinned down in Chapter XXXVIII shows, he still harbors genuine affection for the man.

Like Farfrae's budding romance with Lucetta when Henchard is ready to take Lucetta as his wife, Newson's unexpected arrival at Henchard's house disrupts Henchard's life noticeably. His newfound desire to have a close relationship with Elizabeth-Jane, like his desire to marry Lucetta, constitutes a heavily considered and deliberate change of attitude on his part. The unpredictable obstacle Newson presents to the happiness Henchard seeks with Elizabeth-Jane is made painfully clear by Hardy's melodramatic rendering of Newson's reappearance:

> In truth, a great change had come over [Henchard] with regard to [Elizabeth-Jane], and he was developing the dream of a future lit by her filial presence, as though that way alone could happiness lie.
>
> He was disturbed by another knock at the door. . . .

By juxtaposing Henchard's apparent sole way to happiness and Newson's knocking, Hardy suggests that Newson's intrusion actually disturbs Henchard's "dream of a future." Given the structure of the novel thus far, wherein peripheral characters, such as the furmity-woman, tend to appear at the most inopportune times, Newson's reappearance can only bode ill.

Henchard's selfish and deceitful means of dealing with Newson threaten to rob him of his last bit of self-respect. Despite all this deception, pettiness, and his rabid temper, Henchard remains an essentially sympathetic character. Given his deep, newfound love for Elizabeth-Jane, and the desperateness of his desire to have that love returned, we understand Henchard's deceitful behavior. Like so many of Henchard's decisions, fooling Newson has nothing to do with calculation or manipulation and everything to do with "the impulse of a moment." In this light, Henchard's treatment of Newson is the frantic act of a scared, lonely, and highly pitiable man.

Chapters XLIII–XLV

. . . that no flours be planted on my grave.
& that no man remember me.
To this I put my name.   (See QUOTATIONS, p. 58)

Summary: Chapter XLIII

Henchard continues to worry about what will become of him if
Elizabeth-Jane marries. One day, while spying the spot where
Elizabeth-Jane and Farfrae normally meet, he sees Newson through
his telescope. When Elizabeth-Jane comes home, she has not yet met
Newson, but she tells Henchard that she has received a letter from
someone asking her to meet him that night at Farfrae's house. Much
to her chagrin, Henchard tells her that he has decided to leave Casterbridge that very evening. Elizabeth-Jane believes that he is leaving
because he disapproves of her impending marriage to Farfrae, but
he assures her that such is not the case. Alone, Henchard departs
town. He compares his fate to that of the biblical figure Cain but
declares, "[M]y punishment is *not* greater than I can bear!"

That evening, at Farfrae's house, Elizabeth-Jane meets Newson
and immediately understands the reason for Henchard's sudden
departure. She is overjoyed at her reunion with the father she had
believed dead, but she is upset when she learns of Henchard's deception. Newson and Farfrae begin to plan the wedding.

Summary: Chapter XLIV

Meanwhile, Henchard makes his way through the countryside and
eventually arrives at Weydon-Priors, the very spot where he sold his
wife more than twenty-five years earlier. He reflects briefly upon
those past events and then goes on, settling in a spot some fifty miles
from Casterbridge and finding employment as a hay-trusser. One
day, he speaks to some travelers who have come from Casterbridge
and learns that the wedding between Farfrae and Elizabeth-Jane is
to take place on St. Martin's Day. He decides to go to Casterbridge
for the wedding and sets off on his journey. On the night before the
wedding, he stops in a nearby town and buys some proper clothes
and a caged goldfinch as a present for Elizabeth-Jane.

When Henchard arrives at Farfrae's house in Casterbridge, the
celebration is already underway. As he enters, he leaves the caged
bird under a bush near the back of the house. He watches the dancing unseen, until Elizabeth-Jane's housekeeper informs her that she

has a visitor. She comes in to see him and reprimands him for deceiving her about Newson. So coldly received, he decides to leave and promises never to trouble her again.

SUMMARY: CHAPTER XLV
Several days after the wedding, Elizabeth-Jane discovers the birdcage with a bird—now dead from starvation—inside, and she wonders how it got there. About a month later, after speaking to one of her servants, Elizabeth-Jane figures that Henchard must have brought it as a gift, and she begins to regret the way she treated him. When Farfrae comes home, she asks him to help her find Henchard so that she can make her peace with him. They track Henchard to the cottage of Abel Whittle, who tells them that the man has just died. He gives them a piece of paper that Henchard left, which turns out to be his will. The will stipulates that Elizabeth-Jane not be told about his death, that he not be buried in consecrated ground, that no one mourn for him, and that no one remember him. Elizabeth-Jane regrets her harsh treatment of Henchard the last time they met, and she determines to carry out his dying wishes as best she can.

> *And in being forced to class herself among the*
> *fortunate she did not cease to wonder at the*
> *persistence of the unforeseen. . . .*
> (See QUOTATIONS, p. 59)

ANALYSIS: CHAPTERS XLIII–XLV
In these final chapters, Michael Henchard succumbs to the defeat he has courted throughout the novel. The plot of *The Mayor of Casterbridge* is essentially a series of incidents in which Henchard tries again and again to expunge the guilt he feels for his shameful behavior at the fair at Weydon-Priors. The depth of Henchard's guilt is apparent in many of his actions and emotions: his desperate need to divulge his secret to Farfrae, his determination to remarry a woman he never loved, his willingness to care for Elizabeth-Jane even after he learns that she is not his daughter. Above all, the burden that Henchard bears for his guilt manifests itself in his acceptance of the forces that seem bent upon his destruction.

There is an element of self-destructiveness in Henchard's character. For example, Henchard could have easily denied the accusations of the furmity-woman in the courtroom and spared himself from insult and injury. His willingness to suffer is an important thread in the fabric of his character. His sense of what is right trumps his desire for comfort and makes it impossible for him to live a life he is convinced he has not earned. Henchard believes that he must suffer, as though misery were a means of becoming worthy of such love and comfort. As he leaves Casterbridge, having alienated Elizabeth-Jane and therefore destroyed his last hope of happiness, Henchard compares himself to Cain, the son of Adam and Eve whom God, according to the Bible, condemned to a lifetime of suffering for killing his brother, Abel. His resolute exclamation that, unlike Cain, he can bear his punishment reflects his willingness to do so.

It is through defeat that Henchard becomes a man of true character. His willingness to bear the brunt of his suffering and his continual refusal to foist his misery on others and resist suicide mark him as a hero. Indeed, in many respects, Henchard conforms to the tradition of the tragic hero, a character whose greatest qualities or actions ultimately lead to his or her downfall. In the novel's last chapters, Henchard's determination to spare Elizabeth-Jane any sorrow elevates him into this admirable realm. As he faces a lonely death in a humble cottage, his resolve lies in his desire not to burden any further a world that seems so bent on human suffering. The tragic irony of Henchard's story is that leaving Elizabeth-Jane to live her life in peace is his greatest and most selfless act, proof that he is a man of worthy name and reputation. Instead, the novel ends with the promise of his obscurity. There is no greater punishment for a man whose every struggle has been to secure his public standing than the dictum that he be forgotten; in keeping with his character, Henchard has already embraced this punishment.

Important Quotations Explained

1. The difference between the peacefulness of interior nature and the wilful hostilities of mankind was very apparent at this place. In contrast with the harshness of the act just ended within the tent was the sight of several horses crossing their necks and rubbing each other lovingly as they waited in patience to be harnessed for the homeward journey. Outside the fair, in the valleys and woods, all was quiet. The sun had recently set, and the west heaven was hung with rosy cloud, which seemed permanent, yet slowly changed. To watch it was like looking at some grand feat of stagery from a darkened auditorium. In presence of this scene after the other there was a natural instinct to abjure man as the blot on an otherwise kindly universe; till it was remembered that all terrestrial conditions were intermittent, and that mankind might some night be innocently sleeping when these quiet objects were raging loud.

In Chapter I, after selling his wife and daughter to a sailor for five guineas, Michael Henchard steps out of the furmity-merchant's tent and considers the world described above. Here, Hardy employs his talent for description that serves to make the physical world of the characters real and accessible, while carrying a symbolic meaning that resonates with the larger themes of the work as a whole. First, he evokes beautifully the natural world of Weydon-Priors: the horses, the surrounding woods, the "rosy cloud[s]" at sunset. With the patient horses that rub their necks lovingly and stand as a counterpoint to Henchard's patently unloving treatment of his wife, the passage departs from strict realism and veers toward symbolism. By contrasting the human and natural worlds in this way and determining that "all terrestrial conditions were intermittent," that love and hate, kindness and cruelty are in constant flux, Hardy effectively sets the stage for his drama.

2. He advertised about the town, in long posters of a
   pink colour, that games of all sorts would take place
   here; and set to work a little battalion of men under
   his own eye. They erected greasy-poles for climbing,
   with smoked hams and local cheeses at the top. They
   placed hurdles in rows for jumping over; across the
   river they laid a slippery pole, with a live pig of the
   neighborhood tied at the other end, to become the
   property of the man who could walk over and get it.
   There were also provided wheelbarrows for racing,
   donkeys for the same, a stage for boxing, wrestling,
   and drawing blood generally; sacks for jumping in.

Several times throughout the novel, Hardy evokes details of a kind
of life that was becoming extinct even as he described it. Casterbridge is a town situated between two times: the age of simple, agricultural England and the epoch of modern, industrialized England.
The drama enacted between Henchard and Farfrae is, in part, the
conflict between tradition and innovation, between the past and the
future. Given enough time, the strongest traditions will fade as
surely as memories of the past. Thus, Hardy plays the part of the
amateur anthropologist, recalling rather fondly the details of rural
living that were eclipsed by the advent of modern technologies. In
Chapter XVI, he colorfully describes the day of celebration that
Henchard plans. It is a world of simple pleasures—smoked hams
and local cheeses—a world in which neighbors have not yet suc-
cumbed to the brutal competitiveness of industrial capitalism but
instead share ownership of livestock. It is essentially a romantic and
nostalgic view of a world that, even during Hardy's time, no longer
existed. Nevertheless, Hardy cannot resist including details that
confirm his understanding of the brutality of the universe, as in the
cruelty inherent in such pastimes as "boxing, wrestling, and drawing blood generally."

3. Character is Fate, said Novalis, and Farfrae's
character was just the reverse of Henchard's, who
might not inaptly be described as Faust has been
described—as a vehement gloomy being who had
quitted the ways of vulgar men without light to guide
him on a better way.

This passage from Chapter XVII relates to Farfrae's enormous business success after Henchard requests that he leave his employment
and stop courting Elizabeth-Jane. The phrase "Character is Fate,"
from Novalis, an eighteenth-century German novelist and poet,
offers us a context for understanding much of Henchard's ensuing
struggle. Henchard blames much of the suffering he endures on
cruel forces that are bent on human destruction. In Chapter XVII,
however, Hardy reminds the reader that Henchard has much to do
with his own downfall. In the same chapter, we read that "there was
still the same unruly volcanic stuff beneath the rind of Michael Henchard as when he had sold his wife at Weydon Fair." This "volcanic
stuff" refers to Henchard's passionate disposition. Whatever he
feels—be it love, hate, desire, or contempt—he feels it overpower-
ingly. The same holds true for his guilt over selling Susan, which
tracks him from Weydon-Priors to Casterbridge, where it overshad-
ows his life for twenty years. His desire to right these past wrongs
and his conviction that he deserves to suffer for them account for his
suffering as much as any malignant force of the universe.

QUOTATIONS

4.   MICHAEL HENCHARD'S WILL

That Elizabeth-Jane Farfrae be not told of my death,
or made to grieve on account of me.
& that I be not bury'd in consecrated ground.
& that no sexton be asked to toll the bell.
& that nobody is wished to see my dead body.
& that no murners walk behind me at my funeral.
& that no flours be planted on my grave.
& that no man remember me.
To this I put my name.

MICHAEL HENCHARD

In his introduction to *Modern Critical Interpretations: Thomas Hardy's The Mayor of Casterbridge,* Harold Bloom cites the above passage, taken from the novel's final chapter, as the most powerful and eloquent of all of Hardy's writing. Indeed, there is a remarkable power and beauty in the simplicity of these lines. Henchard's will is the tragic last statement of a tragic man whose unremitting doubts regarding his life's worth not only lead to his death but also follow him there. From the moment Henchard sells his wife at the Weydon fair, he feels a keen anxiety over the value of his name. He pledges a twenty-one-year reprieve from alcohol and sets himself on a course that delivers him to the most honored business and social offices of a small country town. Unsatisfied with this seeming reformation of himself, however, he continues to let his guilt eat away at him and eventually relinquishes the name and reputation he has built for himself. His last wish, to be allowed to die anonymously and to go unremembered, is the ultimate gesture of a man who craves good repute but doubts his own worth.

QUOTATIONS

5.   Her experience had been of a kind to teach her, rightly
     or wrongly, that the doubtful honour of a brief transit
     through a sorry world hardly called for effusiveness,
     even when the path was suddenly irradiated at some
     half-way point by daybeams rich as hers. But her
     strong sense that neither she nor any human being
     deserved less than was given, did not blind her to the
     fact that there were others receiving less who had
     deserved much more. And in being forced to class
     herself among the fortunate she did not cease to
     wonder at the persistence of the unforeseen, when the
     one to whom such unbroken tranquillity had been
     accorded in the adult stage was she whose youth had
     seemed to teach that happiness was but the occasional
     episode in a general drama of pain.

These lines make up the final passage of the novel and provide a
thoughtful, balanced summary of its proceedings. Elizabeth-Jane
decides to honor Henchard's last wishes as best she can. She does
not mourn him or plant flowers on his grave. She does, however,
come close to honoring him inwardly, when she reflects here on the
unfair distribution of happiness, which she considers the most valuable human currency. Her reflection mitigates Henchard's obsession with the worth of his name and reputation, for in the face of
such a "sorry world," all honor seems "doubtful." But it also grants
the fallen mayor a quiet, unassuming kind of forgiveness. She certainly has Henchard in mind when she thinks of the many people
who "deserved much more" out of life. Indeed, given that the world
emerges as "a general drama of pain," both we and Elizabeth-Jane
begin to understand better Henchard's disastrous mistakes and mis-
steps. Even his lie regarding Newson becomes less grievous when we
consider that he meant only to secure a happiness that had, for so
many years, eluded him. In such a bleak world, the course of Henchard's life seems not to merit punishment so much as it does pity.

QUOTATIONS

KEY FACTS

FULL TITLE
: *The Life and Death of the Mayor of Casterbridge: A Story of a Man of Character*

AUTHOR
: Thomas Hardy

TYPE OF WORK
: Novel

GENRE
: Tragedy; naturalism; Bildungsroman (a novel that charts the protagonist's moral and psychological development)

LANGUAGE
: English

TIME AND PLACE WRITTEN
: 1885–1886, Dorchester, England

DATE OF FIRST PUBLICATION
: The novel appeared in serial form concurrently in *Graphic* magazine in England and in *Harper's Weekly* in the United States from January to May 1886. It was first published in book form in 1886.

PUBLISHER
: Smith, Elder (in England); Henry Holt (in America)

NARRATOR
: The anonymous narrator speaks in the third person.

POINT OF VIEW
: The point of view is, for the most part, limited to observations concerning the external world of the characters: how they act, what they see, and what they say. Occasionally an omniscient narrator breaks in to provide necessary information or back story, as in Chapter XXII where the narrator breaks the chronological flow of the story in order to provide essential information about events that occurred the previous night.

TONE
Tragic, melodramatic, naturalistic

TENSE
Past

SETTING (TIME)
Mid-1800s

SETTING (PLACE)
Casterbridge, England (a fictional town based on the city of Dorchester)

PROTAGONIST
Michael Henchard

MAJOR CONFLICT
Wracked with guilt over selling his wife and child, Henchard tries to escape from the shadow of his past and his overwhelming need to punish himself for it.

RISING ACTION
Henchard arranges to remarry Susan.

CLIMAX
The furmity-woman, recognizing Henchard as the man who sold his wife and child at a fair in Weydon-Priors, divulges his shameful secret to the town of Casterbridge.

FALLING ACTION
Having fallen out with Elizabeth-Jane, his only hope for a renewed life, Henchard slinks off to a humble country cottage to die.

THEMES
The importance of character; the value of a good name; the indelibility of the past

MOTIFS
Coincidence; the tension between tradition and innovation; the tension between public life and private life

SYMBOLS
The caged goldfinch; the bull; the collision of the wagons

FORESHADOWING

Farfrae's accumulation of Henchard's business, social position, and family is first foreshadowed by Henchard's failed day of celebration, which takes place alongside the Scotchman's successful party.

STUDY QUESTIONS & ESSAY TOPICS

STUDY QUESTIONS

1. The Mayor of Casterbridge *tells the story of one man's fall and another's rise. Indeed, Henchard's fortune seems inversely proportional to Farfrae's: whatever Henchard loses, Farfrae gains. Is this a believable exchange? If not, is there something more important than realism suggested by Henchard's relationship with Farfrae?*

In terms of realism, the relationship between Henchard and Farfrae seems too finely plotted to be wholly credible. Given Farfrae's charisma, we might believe that he succeeds in winning the heart of Elizabeth-Jane and even in detracting from Henchard's business by winning the hearts of the citizens of Casterbridge. But his successful seduction of Lucetta, his succession to the seat of mayor, his purchase of Henchard's house, and his acquisition of Henchard's furniture convey the feeling that the characters are puppets being conveniently manipulated by the author. The predetermined nature of main characters' reversals of fortunes suggests that realism was not Hardy's first priority. Indeed, the relationship between Henchard and Farfrae carries symbolic weight. When they clash, their disagreement represents a conflict between age and youth, tradition and innovation, and emotion and reason. Henchard, for example, is the mayor of a town that has remained untouched by the scientific, philosophical, or technological advances of the age. Casterbridge exists in a sort of bubble, and Henchard rules it accordingly. He manages his books in his head, conducts business by word of mouth, and employs weather-prophets—already obsolete in many parts of the country—to determine the success of a harvest. When Farfrae arrives, he brings a new system of organization that revolutionizes Casterbridge's grain business, making it more efficient and dependent on developing agricultural technologies. In his proud display of the automatic seeder to a disdainful Henchard, there is clearly more at stake than the friendship between two men.

2. *Discuss the role of coincidence in the novel. Many critics of Hardy have argued that the astonishing coincidences throughout* The Mayor of Casterbridge *make the story improbable and unbelievable. Do you think this is the case?*

By Chapter III, in which Susan Henchard learns her husband's whereabouts from the same furmity-woman who witnessed their shameful parting eighteen years earlier, unlikely coincidences already play an important role in the novel. Such strange occurrences accumulate rapidly: Farfrae, who has a secret for salvaging grown wheat, passes by the Three Mariners Inn just as Henchard cries out for a solution to his damaged crop; Henchard finds the letter revealing that he is not Elizabeth-Jane's father only moments after he pledges his paternal devotion to her; Elizabeth-Jane meets Lucetta Templeman because she strolls past Susan's grave when Lucetta is studying Susan's headstone. These incidents *do* detract from the realism of Henchard's story: no one, not even the most generous reader, could deny Hardy's reliance on outlandish coincidences to propel the narrative. Because many novels were published in serial form, Victorian novelists depended upon such effects in order to hook their readers and boost future sales. In *The Mayor of Casterbridge,* Hardy's plotting relates directly to the plight of his main character: the coincidences that often serve to push the mayor closer to destruction form the machinery of a world bent, as Henchard observes time and again, on human suffering.

3.   *Discuss the role of the peasants of Casterbridge, such as Christopher Coney, Solomon Longways, Nance Mockridge, and Mother Cuxsom.*

The peasants, or rustics, serve two important functions in *The Mayor of Casterbridge*. First, they provide commentary on the actions of the principal characters. In this respect, they act like the chorus in ancient Greek drama, in which bands of actors appeared onstage to comment on the play's events. The rustics congregate after Susan's death and, later, in Mixen Lane where they learn of Lucetta's affair with Michael Henchard. In both scenes, the peasants' commentary provides context for understanding the world of the novel. Christopher Coney's insistence that he is justified in stealing the pennies out of Susan's casket not only testifies to the hardships of the poverty-stricken inhabitants of Casterbridge but also confirms Hardy's measure of the depth of human suffering.

Disturbing as Coney's admission is, however, the scene is a rather comic one. With their colorful dialect and untraditional manners, the rustics lend a bit of welcome comic relief to the novel, even though their second function is serious. Unlike a Greek chorus, which comments on the main action without participating in it, Hardy's rustics play a vital role in the unfolding drama. Nance Mockridge suggests that Lucetta Templeman be publicly chastised for her relationship with Henchard, and soon a "skimmity-ride" sweeps through the town streets, which causes Lucetta enough shame to bring about her death. In this way, the rustics act as one of the uncontrollable (and often malignant) forces that bring about human suffering.

SUGGESTED ESSAY TOPICS

1. Hardy described himself as a determinist—in other words, he believed that the course of human life was shaped by forces, internal or external, beyond human control. Does this philosophy hold true in *The Mayor of Casterbridge*? What forces are responsible for shaping Henchard's life?

2. Is Henchard a tragic character? Why or why not? Does he possess a tragic flaw that leads to his downfall? If so, what is it?

3. Discuss the similarities between Elizabeth-Jane and Farfrae, as well as those between Henchard and Lucetta. What effects does Hardy achieve through these pairings?

4. Is Henchard a sympathetic character? Should we pity him at the end of the novel, or does he seem to get exactly what he deserves?

Review & Resources

Quiz

1. At the opening of the novel, what is Michael Henchard's occupation?

    A. Shepherd
    B. Farmer
    C. Balladeer
    D. Hay-trusser

2. To whom does Henchard sell his wife?

    A. A furmity-seller
    B. A sailor
    C. A farmer
    D. A nobleman

3. The morning after selling his wife, what pledge does Henchard make?

    A. Not to drink for a period of twenty-one years
    B. To search for her and make amends
    C. To chose a better wife for his second marriage
    D. To live the God-fearing life of a good citizen

4. Upon arriving in Casterbridge, where does Susan Henchard predict that she and Elizabeth-Jane will find Henchard?

    A. In the mayor's office
    B. In the stocks
    C. In the town's finest hotel
    D. In a brothel

5. Why does Henchard take such a strong and immediate liking to Donald Farfrae?

    A.   Farfrae is a good drinking companion
    B.   Farfrae helps Henchard avoid an uncomfortable confrontation with Susan and Elizabeth-Jane
    C.   Farfrae shares with Henchard a technique that makes ruined grain usable
    D.   Farfrae provides Henchard with some investment opportunities that promise to earn Henchard a lot of money

6. Who had Henchard arranged to hire as his business manager before meeting Farfrae?

    A.   Christopher Coney
    B.   Solomon Longways
    C.   Nance Mockridge
    D.   Joshua Jopp

7. How does Henchard deal with Abel Whittle's failure to report to work on time?

    A.   He urges the man's wife to wake her husband earlier each morning
    B.   He humiliates the man by sending Whittle into the fields without his pants
    C.   He fires Whittle
    D.   He turns the matter over to Farfrae

8. How is the "day of public rejoicing" that Henchard arranges thwarted?

    A.   He goes on a drinking binge and botches the plans
    B.   The visit of a Royal Personage overshadows the event
    C.   It rains
    D.   Susan takes ill, and Henchard is forced to turn his attentions to her

9. Why does Susan insist on keeping hidden the fact that Elizabeth-Jane does chores in exchange for a room at the inn?

   A. She fears that news of her daughter's duties will reach the mayor and bring shame on him

   B. She is embarrassed by Elizabeth-Jane's clumsiness and awkward manners

   C. After leaving Henchard, Susan lived a life of luxury for a time and believes that doing chores is below her daughter's station

   D. The innkeepers treat Elizabeth-Jane badly, and Susan wishes to spare them from the wrath of the mayor

10. In a letter written on her deathbed, what does Susan confess to her husband?

   A. She and Elizabeth-Jane were abused by the man to whom Henchard sold them

   B. She amassed a great fortune after being sold

   C. Elizabeth-Jane is not his daughter but rather the child of the sailor to whom he sold them

   D. She never loved him

11. Why does Henchard agree to remarry Susan rather than pursue his affair with Lucetta?

   A. He believes that honoring his duties to his first wife is the best thing to do

   B. He does not feel as passionately about Lucetta as he does about Susan

   C. The widowed Susan brings with her more substantial possessions

   D. He feels insecure that because Lucetta is young she will be more likely to fall in love with other men

REVIEW & RESOURCES

12.   Why does Henchard retract his demand that Farfrae no longer court Elizabeth-Jane?

A.   Henchard fears that his failing business ventures will land him in poverty, and he wants to spare Elizabeth-Jane from this fate

B.   After learning the truth about her parentage, Henchard loses his affection for Elizabeth-Jane and hopes that Farfrae will marry and take her away

C.   Henchard realizes that he has been wrongheaded and wishes to mend his friendship with Farfrae

D.   Henchard hopes to join his family to Farfrae's, thereby
connecting himself to the young man's more profitable
business ventures

13.   What is the name of Lucetta Templeman's estate?

A.   The Ring
B.   The Three Mariners
C.   The Royal Arms
D.   High-Place Hall

14.   What ulterior motive prompts Lucetta to invite Elizabeth-Jane to live with her?

A.   She hopes Elizabeth-Jane will ensure frequent visits from Henchard
B.   She has heard that Elizabeth-Jane is a skilled housekeeper and needs help maintaining her estate
C.   She hopes to sabotage Elizabeth-Jane's budding romance with Farfrae
D.   She has no ulterior motives; she is simply lonely and wants the company

15.   Where did Lucetta live before moving to Casterbridge?

A.   London
B.   Paris
C.   Jersey
D.   Weydon-Priors

16. How does Lucetta react when Henchard demands that she end her affair with Farfrae in order to marry him?

    A.   She tells him that she will love whomever she chooses

    B.   She denies having an affair

    C.   Fearing that her reputation will be further damaged by

           scandal, she agrees and gives up Farfrae

    D.   She agrees never to see Farfrae again, but continues their affair behind Henchard's back

17. To whom does Henchard entrust Lucetta's letters?

    A.   Elizabeth-Jane

    B.   Joshua Jopp

    C.   Nance Mockridge

    D.   Dr. Chalkfield

18. What does Henchard persuade the town's musicians to play at the Three Mariners Inn?

    A.   A love ballad that expresses his feelings for Lucetta

    B.   A patriotic song that indulges his drunken sentimentality

    C.   A psalm to which he sets words that expresses his contempt for Farfrae

    D.   A folk song rumored to bring good luck to farmers

19. What is Farfrae's initial reaction when asked to be mayor of Casterbridge?

    A.   He accepts enthusiastically

    B.   He accepts but admits that the position is only a stepping stone for bigger and better things

    C.   He is interested in the position but demands a raise

    D.   He worries that he is too young for the position

20. What is the name of the ceremony the townspeople perform to shame Lucetta?

    A. A harlot's parade
    B. A skimmity-ride
    C. A swoon bumple
    D. A smutting

21. How does Lucetta react to the townspeople's attempt to shame her?

    A. She leaves Casterbridge immediately
    B. She has an epileptic fit and dies
    C. She commits suicide
    D. She scorns them and continues to live her life as she pleases

22. What is Henchard's official role in greeting the Royal Personage?

    A. He has no official role, as Farfrae, the new mayor, has forbidden his participation in the ceremony
    B. He delivers a speech expressing the citizens' gratitude and admiration
    C. He is a flag-bearer
    D. He sings the national anthem

23. What event causes Elizabeth-Jane to sever her ties with Henchard?

    A. She discovers that Henchard is not her biological father
    B. She discovers that Henchard sold her mother at a country fair
    C. She discovers that Henchard stopped her from meeting her biological father by falsely reporting her death
    D. After marrying Farfrae, she decides that she can no longer associate with a common hay-trusser

24. Who cares for Henchard in his dying days?

    A. Dr. Chalkfield

    B. Abel Whittle

    C. Joshua Jopp

    D. No one cares for the fallen mayor, and he dies in obscurity

25. To what biblical figure does Henchard compare himself in his suffering?

    A. Cain

    B. Jesus

    C. Job

    D. Moses

ANSWER KEY:

1: D; 2: B; 3: A; 4: B; 5: C; 6: D; 7: B; 8: C; 9: A; 10: C;
11: A; 12: B; 13: D; 14: A; 15: C; 16: A; 17: B; 18: C; 19: D;
20: B; 21: B; 22: A; 23: C; 24: B; 25: A

SUGGESTIONS FOR FURTHER READING

BLOOM, HAROLD, ed. *Modern Critical Interpretations: Thomas Hardy's* THE MAYOR OF CASTERBRIDGE. New York: Chelsea House Publishers, 1988.

CASAGRANDE, PETER J. *Unity in Hardy's Novels: Repetitive Symmetries.* Lawrence: University Press of Kansas, 1982.

DALESKI, H. M. *Thomas Hardy and the Paradoxes of Love.* Columbia: University of Missouri Press, 1997.

EDWARDS, DUANE D. "*The Mayor of Casterbridge* as Aeschylean Tragedy," *Studies in the Novel.* 4 (1972): 608–618.

GUERARD, ALBERT J. *Thomas Hardy: The Novels and Stories.* Cambridge, Massachusetts: Harvard University Press, 1949.

HOWE, IRVING. *Thomas Hardy.* New York: Macmillan Publishing Co., 1966.

KRAMER, DALE. "Character and the Cycle of Change in *The Mayor of Casterbridge,*" in *Tennessee Studies in Literature,* vol. 16 (Knoxville: University of Tennessee Press, 1971). 111–120.

LERNER, LAURENCE. *Thomas Hardy's The Mayor of Casterbridge: Tragedy or Social History.* London: Sussex University Press, 1975.

MICKELSON, ANNE Z. *Thomas Hardy's Women and Men: The Defeat of Nature.* Metuchen, New Jersey: Scarecrow, 1976.

PATERSON, JOHN. "*The Mayor of Casterbridge* as Tragedy," *Victorian Studies* 3 (1959): 151–172.

TAFT, MICHAEL. "Hardy's Manipulation of Folklore and Literary Imagination: The Case of the Wife Sale in *The Mayor of Casterbridge.*" *Studies in the Novel* 13 (1981): 399–407.

A NOTE ON THE TYPE

The typeface used in SparkNotes study guides is Sabon, created by master typographer Jan Tschichold in 1964. Tschichold revolutionized the field of graphic design twice: first with his use of asymmetrical layouts and sanserif type in the 1930s when he was affiliated with the Bauhaus, then by abandoning assymetry and calling for a return to the classic ideals of design. Sabon, his only extant typeface, is emblematic of his latter program: Tschichold's design is a recreation of the types made by Claude Garamond, the great French typographer of the Renaissance, and his contemporary Robert Granjon. Fittingly, it is named for Garamond's apprentice, Jacques Sabon.

SparkNotes
Test Preparation
Guides

The SparkNotes team figured it was time to cut standardized tests down to size. We've studied the tests for you, so that SparkNotes test prep guides are:

Smarter:
Packed with critical-thinking skills and test-
taking strategies that will improve your score.

Better:
Fully up to date, covering all new features of the tests,
with study tips on every type of question.

Faster:
Our books cover exactly what you need to
know for the test. No more, no less.

SparkNotes Guide to the SAT & PSAT
SparkNotes Guide to the SAT & PSAT — Deluxe Internet Edition
SparkNotes Guide to the ACT
SparkNotes Guide to the ACT — Deluxe Internet Edition
SparkNotes Guide to the SAT II Writing
SparkNotes Guide to the SAT II U.S. History
SparkNotes Guide to the SAT II Math Ic
SparkNotes Guide to the SAT II Math IIc
SparkNotes Guide to the SAT II Biology
SparkNotes Guide to the SAT II Physics

SparkNotes Study Guides: